THE WORLD OF

PostSecret

ALSO BY FRANK WARREN

PostSecret

My Secret

The Secret Lives of Men and Women

A Lifetime of Secrets

PostSecret: Confessions on Life, Death, and God

THE WORLD OF
PostSecret

Frank Warren

WM
WILLIAM MORROW
An Imprint of HarperCollins*Publishers*

HarperCollins books may be purchased for educational, business, or sales promotional use. For information please e-mail the Special Markets Department at SPsales@harpercollins.com.

FIRST EDITION

Designed by Kris Tobiassen of Matchbook Digital

Library of Congress Cataloging-in-Publication Data has been applied for.

ISBN 978-0-06-233901-0

14   15   16   17   18   ID/QT   10   9   8   7   6   5   4   3   2   1

CONTENTS

INTRODUCTION

I started inviting people to anonymously mail me artful secrets in 2004. My goal was to receive 365 postcards. As I write this, I have received more than 1,000,000 from all over the world. The secrets continue to come to my home and I read and keep them all. Each secret feels like a gift, and I am truly grateful to every person who has courageously shared their story.

The project has taken me from Alaska to Australia, sharing secrets at colleges, churches, the TED conference, even the White House. The postcards have been exhibited at more than a dozen museums and galleries, from the American Visionary Art Museum in Baltimore to the Museum of Modern Art in New York City. The PostSecret community has raised over $1,000,000 for suicide prevention programs like HopeLine and IMAlive. The website (www.postsecret.com) has had hundreds of millions of views, and this is the sixth PostSecret book, maybe the last.

It has been five years since the last PostSecret book, and this one is packed with more secrets and stories than any of the others. Like all the PostSecret books, the postcards you will see in these pages appear exactly as they arrived in my mailbox, with the original artwork from the sender. Throughout the book, I have tried to respond to some of your questions about all aspects of the project—including the PostSecret app, the most controversial secrets I've received, and my own secrets. In addition, I share my favorite PostSecret event story and describe a harrowing call I took as a volunteer on the suicide prevention hotline.

As a companion to this hardcover book, we have created a new app called PostSecret Universe that is loaded with additional postcards, secrets from the original PostSecret app, private pictures, recordings, and surprises. This digital companion opens up new and experimental ways for us to share more of the PostSecret story, including a virtual tour of the secret location where I keep all the postcards (www.postsecretuniverse.com).

Even though I still get excited each time I walk to my mailbox to check for secrets, I feel as if it might be time for a change. I would like to find ways to return the secrets to the community so they can continue to pass through hands and change lives. Instead of another book, I can imagine partnering with the right person to create handcrafted boxes that could hold actual postcards and be sold with proceeds going to charity.

Or maybe someone reading this will send me a postcard or letter explaining why he or she is the right person to take over PostSecret. Like Willy Wonka, I could hand over the keys and allow PostSecret a second life.

POSTSECRET
AT A GLANCE

The most frequently used words in the
secrets created with the PostSecret app

Years of PostSecret: 10

Tons of Secrets: 1

Books in Print: 1,300,000

Webby Awards: 7

Visits to Website: 690,000,000

Mailboxes: 2

Dollars Raised for HopeLine: 1,000,000

▼ Performances of *PostSecret: The Show*

■ PostSecret art exhibits

● PostSecret Live! events
(plus events in Alaska, five Canadian provinces, Mexico, England, Ireland, Spain, Australia, New Zealand, Brazil, and South Africa)

my family
is like
a foreign country
to me

We learned
for over fifty
years so we'd
be ready for
each other
when we met.

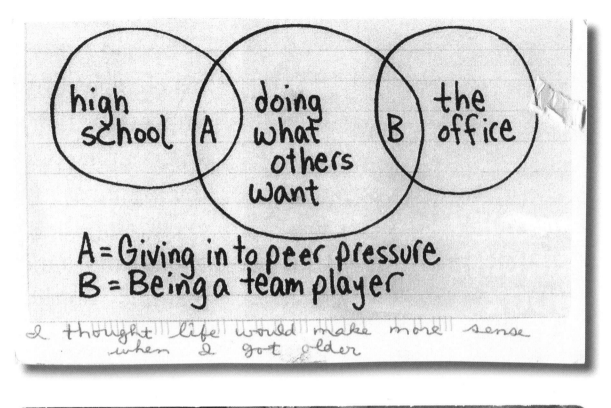

A = Giving in to peer pressure
B = Being a team player

I thought life would make more sense when I got older

During a drunken conversation, my boyfriend confided that as a teen he was involved with a gang.

He killed a person.

I don't feel any differently about him.

The most dangerous snake of all is alarmingly close by.

He dismembered the body and dumped it in a river.

To: THE CREATORS OF **VICODEN**

could I please spend
MOTHER'S DAY
with your mom this year?
You stole mine.

I wrote a post secret
then hid it in my
room to mail later.
Now I can't find it
and am terrified my
Mother did.

Post Secret
13345 Cooper Ridge Rd
Germantown MD 20874

BY AIR MAIL
par avion
Royal Mail®

Royal Mail
Peterborough
Mail Centre
-10-2012
34111264

I kept our sex
tape - not for old times'
sake, but because I
know you'll be important
some day! (SORRY)

PostSecret
13345 Copper Ridge Rd
Germantown
Maryland
20874
U·S·A

At his wedding, my high school sweetheart's mother privately told me she wanted me to marry her son.

Nine years later, I still think about our conversation.

I still love him.

SECRETS ARE THE CURRENCY OF INTIMACY.

I carry a passport and spermicide in my purse always. (just in case the day gets crazy!)

I have this

nagging feeling

that we're

ignoring

something

incredible

Hey JAN,

One of the neighbors said you were having "VISITORS" in the MIDDLE OF THE DAY. So I bought this cute little clock/RADIO/HD VIDEO CAMERA. Finally I have (Proof) And I can

DIVORCE YOU,

P.S. THE Guy you banged... his wife will be getting A copy on her birthday

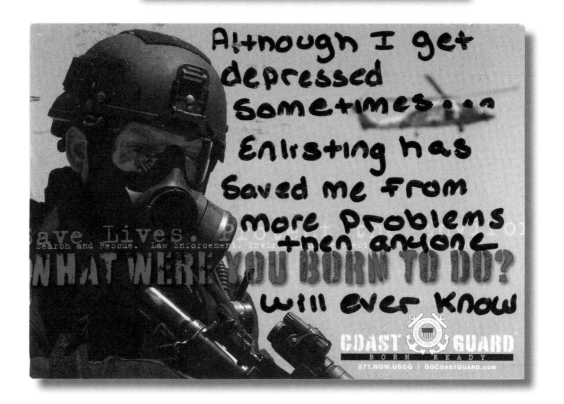

Although I get depressed sometimes... Enlisting has saved me from more problems then anyone will ever know

Save Lives.
Search and Rescue. Law Enforcement. Environment.
WHAT WERE YOU BORN TO DO?
COAST GUARD
BORN READY
877.NOW.USCG | GoCoastGuard.com

I should have died instead of you

I'M Sorry.

I purposely choose a machine in front of a guy so he can watch my ass while I do this:

20

I'm afraid if I tell my husband
I was molested as a child,
he'll think about it every
time we have sex . . .

WE GREW WEED IN HIS MOM'S BACKYARD.

WHEN SHE ASKED WHAT IT WAS, WE SAID,

"I THINK THAT'S A WEED."

I try to work every Thanksgiving so some people will have the chance to spend time with their family, as mine is no longer together.

Even though at the time I was willing, now looking back, it seems like she raped me & robbed me of my virginity.

(I'm taking it back now. It was never hers)

I exaggerated my RAPE because I didn't think anyone would care that he just made me BLOW him.

I've never felt more alone
        than I did just after my rape.

I've never felt less alone
        than I did when one of the people I
    supervise at work, a 72-year-old
woman, offered to go with me to my post-rape
    gynecologist appointments.

    THANK YOU.

After visiting Madrid for the first time in 2007, I saw this postcard and realized that I, too, left my heart in this beloved city. I vowed then that I would find the place in the picture and return in search of my heart.

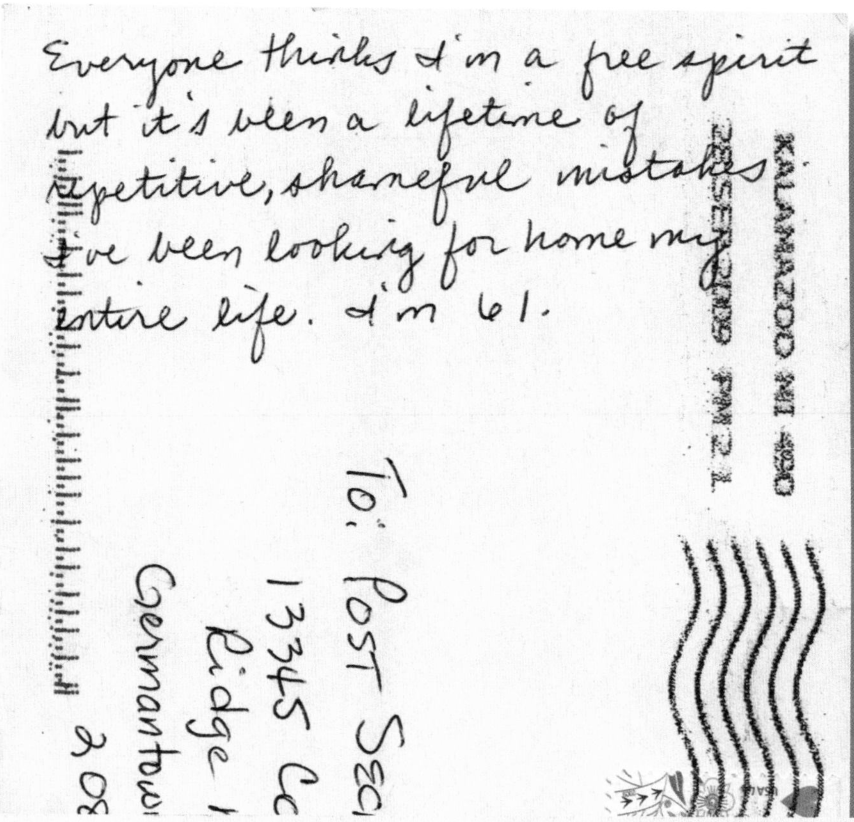

Everyone thinks I'm a free spirit
but it's been a lifetime of
repetitive, shameful mistakes.
I've been looking for home my
entire life. I'm 61.

KALAMAZOO MI 490
28 SEP 2009 PM 2 L

To: Post Sec
13345 Co
Ridge
Germantow
208

Inventure Place
National Inventors Hall of Fame
Akron, Ohio

AKRON OH 443
10 OCT 2006 PM 1 T

USA 24

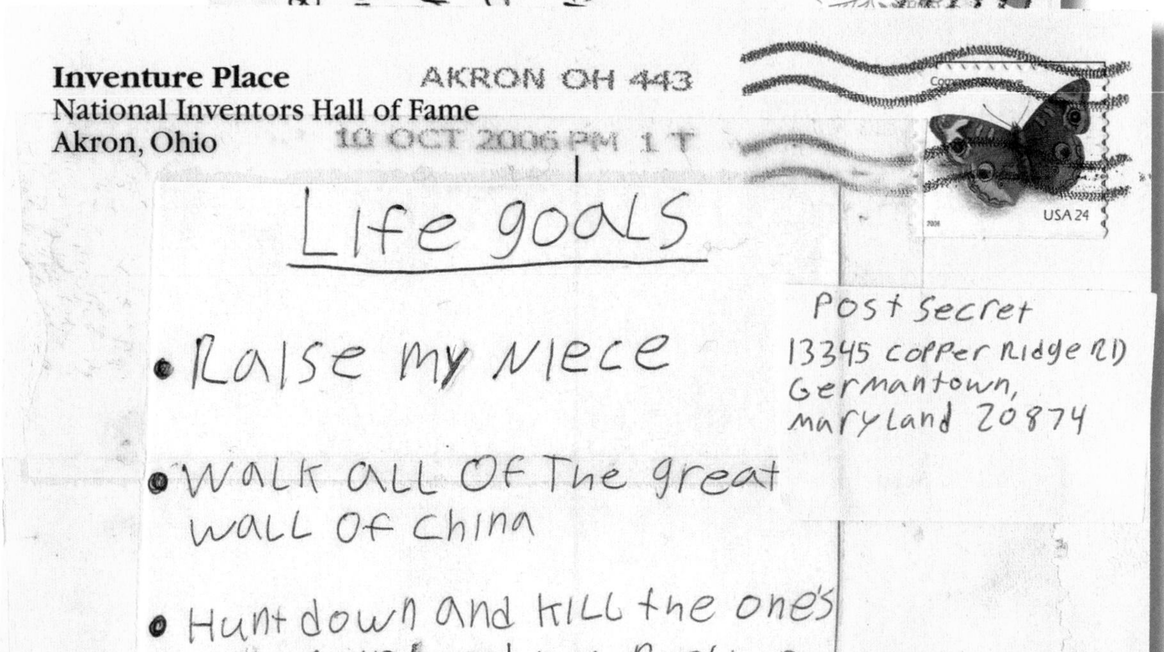

Life goals

- Raise my niece
- Walk all of the great wall of China
- Hunt down and kill the one's who murdered my Brother

Post Secret
13345 Copper Ridge Rd
Germantown,
maryland 20874

Discover the Inventor in You!
Photo Credit: Bruce Ford, City of Akron

When we were talking on the way home, you asked when the happiest moment in my life was. All I wanted to say was, "Now."

I LOVE AND MISS MY EX-HUSBAND TOO SCARED TO TELL HIM

I lied about a major injury in my early teens. It became so real, even I believed it. Now I wonder... would my life be different if I had told the truth?

IN THE COURSE OF MY DUTIES AS A SWORN CORRECTIONS OFFICER, I FRISK SEARCH TENS AND SOMETIMES HUNDREDS OF INMATES DAILY...

(i never want to touch another human being ever again for the rest of my life)

I am afraid to write for fear of what I might discover about myself.

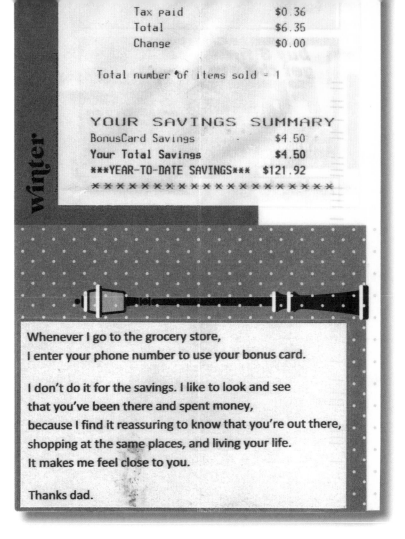

```
        Tax paid              $0.36
        Total                 $6.35
        Change                $0.00

        Total number of items sold = 1


      YOUR   SAVINGS   SUMMARY
    BonusCard Savings         $4.50
    Your Total Savings        $4.50
    ***YEAR-TO-DATE SAVINGS***  $121.92
    * * * * * * * * * * * * * * * * * * *
```

winter

Whenever I go to the grocery store,
I enter your phone number to use your bonus card.

I don't do it for the savings. I like to look and see
that you've been there and spent money,
because I find it reassuring to know that you're out there,
shopping at the same places, and living your life.
It makes me feel close to you.

Thanks dad.

It took my husband 2 years to convince me to join "The Lifestyle"...

...and 2 months for me to fall in love with his best friend.

Post Card

I try to be a good person, but there's a side of me that's just a mean little bitch. I keep her at bay with cookies.

Post Secret
13345 Copper Ridge Rd
Germantown, MD 20874

Today   Jun 11   11:11 AM

I saw his notes for his big proposal plans and a video of the engagement ring on his phone. But now I wish I could tell him not to do it because I love him but I'm not sure I should say yes and I don't want to break his heart.

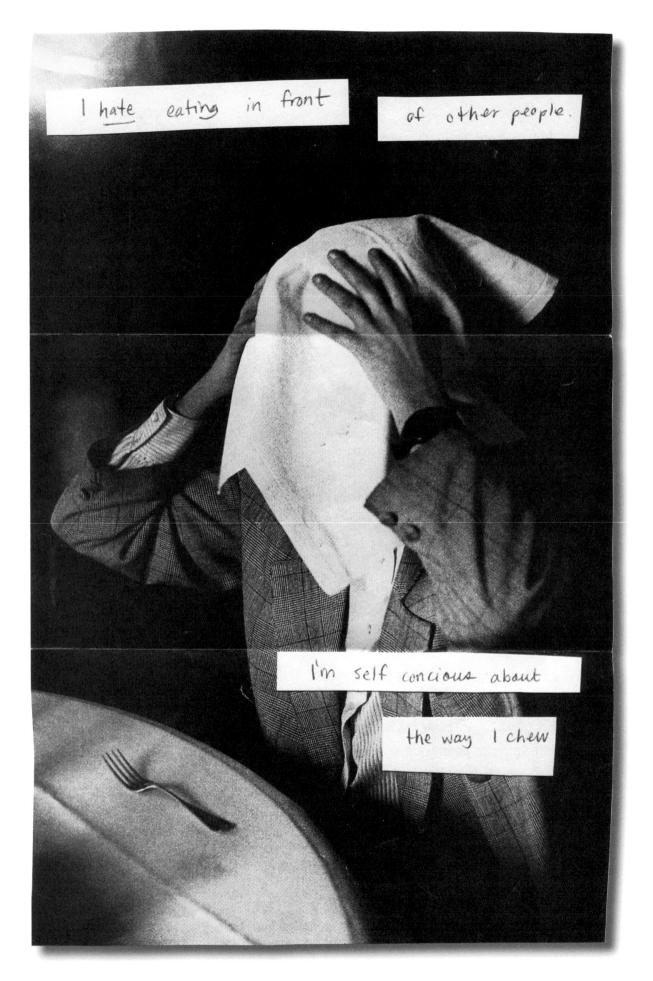

YOGA MAKES ME QUEEF!

I'VE WANTED TO HAVE SEX WITH LITTLE BOYS EVER SINCE I WAS ONE.

(I JUST BEGAN MY SIXTH DECADE OF VIRGINITY.)

I've gone from a full, furnished house, to a backpack full of belongings.

I'VE FOUND HOME.

It was with me the whole time.

It just got lost in all the stuff I had.

JUN · 65

Marrying him was a mistake.

I've lost everything...

including myself.

San Francisco

I made a huge mistake....

I WANT TO COME HOME....

I would leave EVERYTHING behind...

if you asked me to come to San Francisco with you.

THE POSTSECRET APP

Frank, what was the deal with the PostSecret app, and why did you have to kill it?

In the fall of 2011, the PostSecret app was born. When it was released, it was the top-selling app in the United States. For the first time, you could take a picture with your smartphone, type a secret on it, tag it with your general location, and share it with the world.

Tens of thousands of people began creating and responding to these digital secrets every day. They searched for secrets created near them and sometimes replied with a message of hope or a secret of their own. These confessional voices sometimes became conversations uncovering hidden humor or the truth that we are never really alone with our secrets. Surprisingly, some of these anonymous secrets led to acts of kindness and connection in the real world. One of these inspiring stories took place in Brighton, England. (You can read the whole story on page 222).

But soon a determined handful of saboteurs worked to bring down the app by bombing the site with Tiger-Text sex requests and bullying comments. Just three months after its release, I decided to close down the PostSecret app because it was no longer a safe place to share secrets.

Anonymity worked on the PostSecret website but proved to be the Achilles' heel for the app. We were unable to manage the vast number of secrets that were being created every second, day and night, or identify those breaking the community rules. Following the PostSecret app, other apps have experimented with an-

onymity and struggled with similar challenges.

Ending the PostSecret app was painful for me, but the community's last spontaneous act of generosity was a special gift I'll never forget. When I voluntarily closed the app, I promised every user I would personally mail them a full refund if they wanted one. My wife and I had no idea how much this would end up costing us.

Only a handful of people asked for their money back, but letters began to flood my mailbox. I read story after story from people thankful for how the app had changed their lives. A few told how a romantic proposal or marriage was made possible through the app. I was deeply moved by these letters of appreciation, but there was more—I found checks, gift cards, and cash inside the envelopes. The final act of the community was to make sure I would not have to pay a single refund out of my pocket, and I never did.

My wife and I spread some of these kind letters out on our dining room table and took this picture just days after Christmas. It felt like a scene from *It's a Wonderful Life*.

11:18
Friday, August 12

Mom
I'm coming to pick you up Sam tried to kill himself.

This was the scariest moment of my life.

 slide to unlock

I love getting stoned and doing stupid shit with my roommates.

I always tell guys I've never had an orgasm, it always makes them try really hard to be the first :)

 LEVITTOWN
I'm one of "the bravest", my secret? I'm just as afraid of dying in a fire as the people I save.

FIREFIGHTER

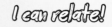

I can relate!

I will never again get to poop in peace.

We don't have the heart to tell her she's not a lap dog..

I couldn't stop crying this morning.
And then my dog walked out of my closet stuck in a clothes hanger.
I don't know where I would be without him.

<3

We are sitting in the ICU waiting room. Grandma had a massive stroke. Thanks for the first laugh in two days.

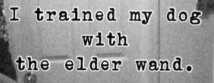

I trained my dog with the elder wand.

You've hit me for the last time. I'm packing my things and leaving you while you're at work.

And I'm taking the dog too!

Always take the dog.

Thank you everyone :)
We are staying with my mom and will get peaceful nights from now on.

I used to be a little bit racist, until my grandson taught me how to love

I use the term "penetrate" as often as possible in formal business occasions. I think it's hilarious to say when nobody can laugh.

See the world :
Cathedral Cove
Whitianga
New Zealand

See the world :) a double rainbow in spring grove, pa

See the world:
Australian Clouds :)

To the person trying to see the world through PS, this is a Hollywood movie set (That's Daniel Day-Lewis as Abraham Lincoln, on a break)

my dream was to travel the world, but a malignant tumor will likely kill me within the next month. My new dream is to see the world through the eyes of Post Secret.

please help me.

Albums | **Camera Roll**

I love the See the World thing going on...

I've taken a screen shot of all the places I wanna go :)

1510 Photos

See the World:
Machu Picchu
Peru

See The World:
Hogwarts

Welcome to
Blue Earth

See the world: Blue
Earth, MN

See the world - Tian Tan Buddha, Lantau Island, Hong Kong

See the world: Gaspereau Valley, Nova Scotia, Canada. My hometown <3

See the world:
Great Wall of
China, Beijing

See the world:
Burning Man

For the person wanting to
see the world.

This is Miyajima, Japan!

To the person who
wants to see the
world: this is
Fairbanks Alaska

For the person who
Wants to see the world
Tumbler Ridge, BC
Canada

I'm really enjoying the "see the
world" pics. Feels good knowing
we're all over this world, and
this app makes us all feel a
little closer.

See the world:
Tel Aviv, Israel
תל אביב, ישראל

SEE THE WORLD.

Dubbo, New South
Wales, Australia.

See the world:
Batavia Illinois:)

To the person trying to see
the world via PS:
My home in Germany

See the world: Zurich,
Switzerland

See the world:
Singapore

See the world:

One tired mamas view in salt
lake city, Utah.

I only like to sit on the front half of planes because the back half got fucked on Lost.

I'm not voting for my husband in the upcoming elections.

He spends too much time at work, the kids need their dad.

Every time I poop I'm scared my baby will fall out. And yes, I realize that is completely irrational..

My adopted son has decided to go live with his bio mom in Florida. I'm hiding notes in all his clothes so he remembers how much I love him! My heart is breaking!!

I think they'll
last forever.

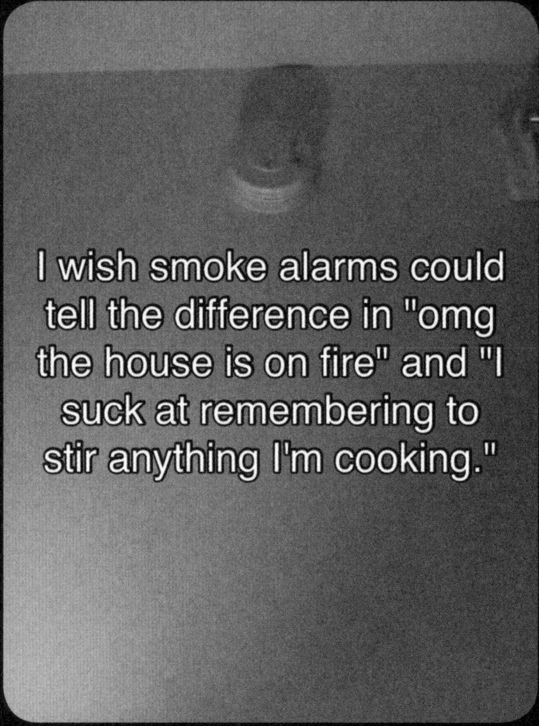

I wish smoke alarms could tell the difference in "omg the house is on fire" and "I suck at remembering to stir anything I'm cooking."

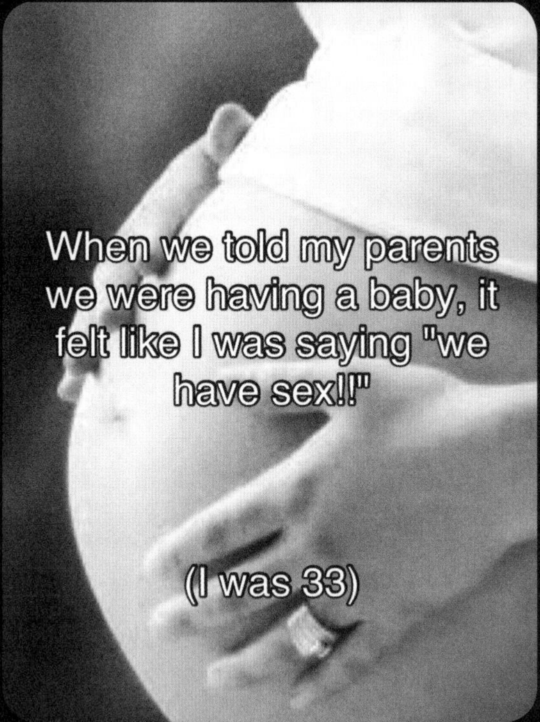

When we told my parents we were having a baby, it felt like I was saying "we have sex!!"

(I was 33)

There's enough data on my phone to end three marriages.

MICHIGAN STATE ™

I told a little girl that my scars were from the tooth fairy. I'm probably going to hell.

I don't care how many bags I have.

I make only 1 trip.

We defend our country with our lives, but the closest I have come to dying today was the moment I leaned too far back in my chair.

Get back to work

Im in the millitary i ask this girl out and this is how i did it she said yes

His parents gave me his dog tags after he was killed in Iraq. Sometimes I laugh when I wear them because I know he approves of being so close to my boobs..and for that split second of a laugh it hurts a little less.

Messages XXXXXXXXXX Clear

I'm gay....

That's okay... BTW WHO IS THIS?

You're just a random number I typed in. I had to practice telling people.

Alright well.. good luck. You can do this

Thank you for Send

giving me courage.

Q W E R T Y U I O P
A S D F G H J K L
Z X C V B N M

Messages wanted to see what I Edit

Call   FaceTime   Add Contact

Text Message

would get. I probably shouldn't have tripped out but damn, really?

I'm gay.

Who is this

You don't know me. I just needed to practice telling people that.

Dont text me any more. Its ur deal

Alright damn I was planning on texting you all the time. Go fuck yourself .

My cheating husband got the house in the divorce. So I put salmon roe inside the curtain rods and screwed the ends back on. He wants to sell now but can't because of the mystery stench. :)

I just noticed I still drive with my hand in "holding yours" position.

Huh. Could've done without that realization.

My wealthy husband has been divorced 7 times because he found out they were only with him for his money.

He married me because he thinks I'm different. I'm not.

This was taken two days after my daddy passed. I made us matching bracelets so we'd always be connected.

I put on a fake engagement ring when I bought the pregnancy test so the cashier didn't judge me.

While secretly taking this photo, my flash went off. So awkward haha

Dear Frank:

It's sad that you had to close the app, but before you did I was able to meet someone—a beautiful woman from Australia. I'm currently at the airport in Dublin, Ireland, waiting for my flight to Australia. I've found love on the other side of the world.

Dear America,

I hope you enjoyed your Tuesday,

Wednesday has been great so far, you're going to enjoy it :)

Love from Australia

Dear Australia,

I hope you're enjoying tomorrow, we are taking care of yesterday for you.

Love,
The United States

He asked me to send him a picture of me getting naked. I sent him this.

I've been sitting here listening to these people make fun of me for 40 minutes.

Should I let them know I speak Vietnamese?

I sometimes think my dog looks like Kim Kardashian.

I like having lunch by myself. I'd rather do that than meet up with any of you most days.

This is my dad. I dressed up as an elf & went around to hospitals passing out candy canes to ppl who won't be home for Xmas. Our secret? We're Jewish! Happy holidays PS!

11:11

Friday, November 11

I saw a news clip on how there have been a bunch of anonymous people who have been taking care of other peoples lay away. The newscaster said its believed to have been started by an iPhone app. I've never felt more proud of this community.

slide to unlock

I wish the people who clean my office at night were invited to our company Christmas party today. They're employees too! (one of them is my Uncle)

I won the ugly christmas sweater contest at a party last night. I didn't even know there was a contest. :(

Tonight I went Xmas shopping with my dad. I saw a daughter on her fathers shoulders and nostalgically said "remember when we used to do that!" I'm 20. he got down on one knee and I rode on his shoulders laughing until a mall cop ran us down yelling at us. My dad is my hero, always will be.

Dear Jesus, As an atheist I'm pretty sure you're not the son of god. That being said you were a pretty cool guy, what with the forgiveness and love. So Happy Birthday, dude. ;)

A few days ago I posted about not being able to afford the American Girl doll my daughter wanted for Christmas. A total stranger from PS got in touch with me and sent my baby girl a doll! There are good people in this world. Thanks EP... I hope you see this.

I just committed my husband to the psych ward. Merry Fucking Christmas

I find more spiritual comfort in libraries than I ever have in any church.

Am i the only one who feels like there is a lot of sexual tension in libraries?

The day he was found not guilty, I wept for hours.

He should have been sent to prison.

The secret? I was his lawyer.

My schizophrenia got me on the Best Seller's list.

My pathological lying wrote me a story.

If a high school teacher sees me in public and calls me by my name 8 years after they taught me, it reinforces what an amazing teacher they were

You're having a tough time. I'm about to knock on your door after flying across the country to surprise you. I told you I'm here for you. Literally.

I spent £8,500 on plastic surgery so my mum didn't see the face of her rapist every time she looked at me.

I'm not him.

My mom just ran into a student she had her first year as a teacher--in 1972!! Mom remembered her first and last name. :)

Me and my mate put our hard skin foot shavings along with parmesan cheese on her ex-boyfriends spag-bol after he cheated on her – revenge is a dish best served hot

I slept with someone, fully knowing the fact that they were on the list of America's Most Wanted.

I left secrets on sticky notes inside these books. Don't tell! ;)

LIFETIME OF SECRETS
FRANK WARREN

POSTSECRET
13345 COPPER RIDGE RD
GERMANTOWN MD
20874-3454

Ever since I became a vegan, vegetarians look like hypocrites (sorry!)

I have been pinched, kicked, yelled at, spit on, peed on, coughed on, pooped on, sneezed on.....yelled at, called the worst names ever... But at the end of the day, i still love what I do...

I have been pinched, kicked, yelled at, spit on, peed on, coughed on, pooped on, sneezed on.....yelled at, called the worst names ever... But at the end of the day, i still love what I do...

Me too. And i'm a preschool teacher.

I wear my panda suit when I'm sad and do chores.

Bad feelings gone:)

It stays like this til I have company.

It's been 10 months, and I'm recovering well. Last night I started crying, looking online at yoga for people like me. I think I focused so hard on recovering that I've never really grieved.

If you tailgate me, I drive slower to piss you off.

Dear cheating husband: Your wife didn't steal the housekeeping key. I gve it to her so she could catch you .

REMOVE KEY
REMUEVA LA
RETIREZ LA CL
SCHLÜSSEL ENTFERNEN
カード を一度 抜き 差す。
取出钥匙

TURN HANDLE
GIRE EL TIRADOR
TOURNEZ LA POIGNÉE
TÜRGRIFF DREHEN
ドアの 握り を 回し ます。
旋转手柄

Dear hotel guest that stripped the bed and saved me 3mins thank you so much!! Have a great holiday!! :)

Messages **Mom** Edit

Ever since she got her iPhone, my mom is addicted to sending me pictures of the cat.

Messages XXXXXXXXXXXXXX Edit

2011-12-14 2:37 PM

I laughed so hard! My mom does too. I thought I was the only one!

"I'm so squished!" 😳

If we didn't loose her, we would still be together. I would Still be together

After my stepdad does the laundry, I put some of my clothes in my mom's basket so it appears as though my stepdad couldn't tell our clothes apart. My mom has been struggling with her weight & I just want her to feel better.

My mum casually slips adorable letters into my lunch container and it brightens up my day! Here's one:

DONT EVER FORGET HOW MUCH I lOVE YOU HAVE A FANTASTIC DAY LOVE MUM

My wife left me a dirty note in my lunch. It was awesome....

My husband packs me the lunch my mom never did.

Make secret:
I will always vow to be the type of man I want my future daughter to fall in love with

Killing a wild dog that attacked me in Iraq effected me more than killing a person.

Dear my future teachers, if you're an ass to me, I photoshop your face and put it all over campus. Don't piss off a graphic designer.

How awesome it would be to have an aerial view of all of us right now. All laying in bed with the glow of postsecret on our faces, reading and connecting to the
Exact
Same
Thing

At least my dog is sleeping! It's 3:44 AM in MD.

No sleep again last night. Please be patient with me.

Are there other insomniacs out there tonight?

The truth about my insomnia is, i can't sleep without you!

Insomnia sucks.

Insomnia

My secret is that I masturbate every night before I go to sleep. Great orgasms are the only cure I could find for insomnia.

I can't sleep. So I'm watching my cat sleep with envy. Insomniacs of the world unite on PS!

Insomnia haunts me.

I lie about my insomnia so they don't worry...

2:03

& b/c I don't want to tell them the cause.

Hey Frank—

When the PostSecret app first came out, I posted a secret that had a picture of 2 driver's licenses. One had a picture of me taken in 2004, when I had a cocaine and prescription painkiller addiction; the other was me in 2011, now five years sober. My secret got a lot of support and I hoped that seeing the difference in my appearance and health would inspire others.

Today—one day after the app was closed—I went to a convenience store to buy cigarettes. When I produced my driver's license, the clerk stared at it for a second, then asked if I had the PostSecret app. At first I panicked and considered lying—but then I said yes, and asked if she'd seen my secret. She pulled out her phone and showed me a screenshot of it. Turns out she had an addiction to painkillers as well, and when she saw my "before" and "after" pictures she saved it as inspiration, and got help. She looks at it every day.

Thanks to your app, I have not only made a new friend (we are going out for lunch later this week!) but have been able to help someone with their struggle with addiction. I understand why you closed the app and respect your decision completely, but I wanted you to know that it brought people together and saved lives. Thank you.

I'm the nanny. I saw her first steps. Her mom is wonderful, she deserved to see them. So when she excitedly told me a week later that her baby walked for the first time, I let her believe it. I feel guilty, but I could never take that away from a mother. I'm sorry.

Every single time I shower, I blow my nose right into my hands and let the water rinse it away. Does anyone else?

One of the old ladies (mid 70s) sitting behind me at this cafe is talking about her husbands penis enlargements lol

I always pretend to do my homework at my college cafeteria so people think its my choice to eat alone.

I'm sitting at school eating lunch right now, and all I can think is "How do anonymous strangers understand me better than anyone here?"

Today I went out for lunch and when I paid I also paid for the lady behind me. This is the happiest I've been in a long time!!

To the cute, sweet, innocent, little 6 year old girl I pulled out of that car last night.

You saved me more than I saved you.

My dog jumps in my pants whenever I take a shit.

She isn't allowed on the bed. (his rule) but once she hears his car leave in the morning for work she knows she is allowed on the bed then. It's our little secret :)

I long for the day I meet a woman and tell her I am an atheist and she will respond, "Hey, me too."

Haha, my neighbours are selling their house and forgot to take their handcuffs off the bed before taking pictures for the sales paper.

My daughter cut her hair for Locks of Love, but we keep putting it in random places just for fun.

I am most scared of people finding out how many times I have viewed their profiles

facebook

I'm a "meter maid". When I'm in other cities and on my days off, I look for meters that are about to expire and put money in them.

Everytime I drive past a strip club i scream DAD! Hoping that the guy walking in will feel horrible and run away :)

I really have to poop. There's someone in the stall next to me clearly waiting for me to leave so she can do the same.

It's become a pooping standoff. This may be the most awkward moment of my life.

I promised her she wouldn't die in pain.

I'm a nurse, I could lose my license and probably go to prison but I kept my promise.

That... Is actually a tupperware container.

Having breast cancer does not make me less of a man.

Ever since he died, I secretly gave up on being a better Christian.

I'm an adult
I live alone
I installed a slide
It's fast
Life is short, enjoy it

(though I do tell visitors
that the previous owner
had kids)

My "family emergency"
this afternoon is hotel sex
with this freak. Secret:
she's my wife and best
friend and I'm still madly
in love after 19 years.

I lost my dad to Parkinson's
June 21st 2011

He never really smiled in
pictures. Even though I looked
like an idiot, I'm glad I made him
smile in this one.

I still play our
numbers for
revenge. When I
win I'm not
sharing.

As a kid, I honestly thought the saying went "awfully wedded wife" instead of "lawfully wedded wife".

I said YES!

To being happy and single.

The only thing I can work in my kitchen is the coffee pot. I can even make spaghetti.

My family thinks I'm dead.

I'm finally free.

The most incredible moment of my life to date, was over-hearing my grandma whisper into my grandpa's ear "you fought hard enough Dadio, it's okay to let go..."

I sleep naked.

One of my biggest fears is having my home invaded at night and having to defend myself in the nude

My phone fell on my face three seconds after I took this picture.

I always thought 'what idiots' when I saw posts about people dropping their phones on their faces reading PS in bed.

Tell you what, it bloody hurts!

Frank—

I don't know if you'll actually read this, but I'll try. I thought you'd like to hear a heartwarming story that resulted from the PostSecret app.

During the last week of the app's existence, someone posted a "secret" saying that she was looking for her half sister, who she'd never met. She gave some basic information and asked the PS community to help. I am a professional researcher and couldn't resist a plea like this, so I hunted around a bit on the web.

I very quickly discovered that the poster's sister had responded to a request the poster had left on a website where people can search for lost relatives. The only problem was that the original poster had left her message in Nov. 2010, and the sister had not found it until Dec. 2011. By the time the sister posted her response, the poster was no longer checking the website. Fortunately, the sister was just as eager to make the connection as the original poster.

I took a screenshot of the sister's response and posted it to the PS app. Fortunately the original poster saw it and e-mailed her sister.

Yesterday I received an e-mail from the poster saying that she and her sister had indeed connected and are now e-mailing each other daily. They hope to meet next summer—she is in Illinois and her sister is in Virginia. She thanked me for the "priceless gift" I had given both of them.

Babysitting for her saved me from prostitution.

And she doesn't have a clue.

For whoever might need this today...

1-800-273-8255 National Suicide Prevention Lifeline

We are all here for you

Your hands will Never hurt Me Again GOODBYE

Every night when I tuck my son in to bed. I whisper in his ear "you saved my life"

I got the idea for this from postsecret.com

It got me laid.

~~...~~ you're ~~...~~ extremely hot.

I get road rage grocery shopping

I secretly convinced my wife to name our son Luke.

Just so I can say 'Luke I am your father'

I hid behind the shower curtain so I could jump out and scare my friend, but he sat down and started pooping and talking to himself. It was so awkward. I just kept hiding.

He's not my baby brother like we tell everyone...

He is my son, but I knew that at 14 I was too young to raise a baby, so my mother saved us.

I called my best friend, and only remembered when a woman answered that he was dead. She listened and talked to me for more than an hour. The next week, she rang me, and we've been friends for three years now.

I have only just found out that 'duck tape' is infact called 'duct tape'

TWIN B   TW

They are the product of my rape... I hope I can love them.

I'm a graffiti artist and I should have been busted twice about a year ago. The cops I talked to thought my art was amazing. They told me to keep doing what I do best.

ANTOINE DE SAINT-EXUPÉR

El Principito

con las acuarelas originales del autor

Every time
I'm far away
from home
I buy this book
and I read it
in a new language.

My brother raped his girlfriend.

I'm sitting behind her family at the trial.

I posted a secret about being scared to testify against my rapists in court. I did it, and I have never felt so strong. The looks on their faces as I pointed at them and told my story was priceless. I'm a survivor not a victim.

Hey Frank,

*It's days like today that I sincerely miss the PostSecret app.
Early on I posted a secret about being scared to go to court and
received nothing but inspirational and encouraging words from
the other users.*

*I wanted to thank you for giving me a sense of strength and sense
of being to know I am not alone, and even if they are strangers,
they believe in me, which made me believe in me.*

*I am currently awaiting the second part of the trial, and have no
doubt in my mind that I'm going to go in there with this strength
and the spirit of the PostSecret community within me.*

My girlfriend was raped 5 months ago and fell pregnant. She told me tonight she's scared I'll leave because of how the baby was conceived. What she doesn't know is I have a ring and tomorrow I'm going to ask her to marry me so we can raise this baby together as a family. Sssh it's a secret!

I will reply to everyone who commented individually later but for now....
She said YES!!!
We're going to be a family!!

I had a orgasm while I was been raped. Does that make me a bit sick too? I can't forgive myself ever.

If I have to brake, your lane change was not successful.

I flash my headlights at other cars to warn them a police car is up ahead.

My boyfriend used my laptop & forget to clear the history so I found out he likes porn of girls peeing themselves. I'm not annoyed but just to mess with him I keep saying things like 'I'm totally gonna pee myself if I don't find a bathroom'! LOL.

I recently got a job as a full time babysitter. The parents don't know that I am their adopted daughters birth mom. I didn't know either until I saw her baby picture was the one I sent them before they adopted her.

I wear an AC/DC shirt under my clergy robes.

I faked sick to get out of work for a couple days, I convinced everyone I was sick even my husband. Today he wakes up saying he is sick and I "gave it to him"

I just attempted suicide...

I'm never doing that again, I almost killed myself!

I was brushing my teeth naked after showering. My cat loves strings of any kind... My reaction has made her hide under the couch for the last hour.

He didn't check the box.

Merry Christmas, y'all!

I have a stutter. The hardest thing for me to say is my name when ordering coffee... So It really hurts when the cashier laughs or says things like "you don't know your own name?" Of course I know my name but please be patient. I can't help it sometimes.

9 years off cocaine. Went to school, became a teacher, got my masters, now im a high school principal.

Someone from my past saw me and asked "what the hell are you doing as a principal"? My answer, helping kids like me.

A book commits suicide every time a young girl says Kim Kardashian is a role model.

I accidently saw my boyfriend's internet history today. You'd think that there would be porn. Instead there was, "little gifts to give to your girlfriend".

Without realizing it. I leaned back on my computer chair after being bored on Facebook, and grabbed my cell phone to check Facebook...

My birth-grandmother had to wait three decades to give me the baby picture of me that she carried every day since my birthmom gave me up. I was ALWAYS loved.

I was adopted and I am so thankful that my birthmom was willing to give me up. I have an amazing life.

It was hindering our marriage, I sold it with all my games and purchased my wife a spa package. Now that's the "call of duty"

My husband knows that I was molested.

What he doesn't know is that it was my sister who molested me.

If I run out of breath doing something stupid (like running up stairs) I will breathe as silently as possible to avoid judgment from others.

I remember how shocked I was when someone said women can become addicted to porn. And then I became one.

I shouldn't be outing him....

But I'm pretty sure he's gay!

I take the Toronto subway. Every day I thought, What if I just jumped? *One night I was lying in bed reading the PostSecret app. I saw* my *secret. Someone posted a TO subway stop stating they wanted to jump too. I posted my stop & wrote* I won't if you won't. *They shortly replied,* deal. *I'm not out of the woods yet, but I will always have that pact I made.*

I've given up on life, but instead of killing myself, I'm running away to Europe to start a new one

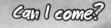

Can I come?

I like to flash the security cameras at work.

Sometimes, if my dog refuses to eat, I pretend to cook his food on the stove. Works every time!

I just wanted someone to see it. Before I took it down. Cuz I got bailed on tonight.

The other day i mentioned to my boyfriend that i didn't understand guys' obsession with boobs. He replied "for the same reason girls love dicks."

I didn't have the heart to tell him most girls find them ugly and weird.

My secret? I didn't join the Army to protect America and yours and my own freedom.

I joined because it was the best paying job I could find. I'm sorry, but it's true.

Last night I dreamed that Frank opened a pizzeria in my town and all of the pizzas had secrets on them instead of toppings.

There is one more secret about the PostSecret app that very few people know. I only uncovered this mystery recently while searching the archive to select app secrets for this book.

For years the app has not been available for purchase and the archive—where all the digital secrets are stored—has been closed. But somehow a small group of users found a way to continue making secrets and send them into the dormant database.

Only I can enter and explore this private archive. It's impossible for others to see any of the secrets stored there, so I was surprised when I discovered these mute confessions being added every day.

Why are people still using the app this way? What does it feel like to write a secret on a postcard and then burn it before it can be seen? Do these secrets tell a different story?

For the first time, here are some of those secrets out of the darkness.

POSTSECRET UNIVERSE

See more app secrets that we couldn't fit into the book.

www.postsecretuniverse.com

Frank, thank you for everything—this incredible place to share our secrets. Goodbye. For now... :) I know nobody can see this. But I'm sending it regardless because of this magical thing called Hope. Yeah, I'll never delete this app.

Yeah, I do plan on proposing at that concert.. Good thing you can't see this ;)

I can't fathom the anger or the violence.

But I can relate to the loneliness and isolation.

Baby Nicholas Cage

I want my money back

I'm posting secrets.
Even if no one
sees them
Maybe *especially*
because no one sees
them
I'M HERE

سسئمتُ الآنتظارَ الطويلَ
بِلا أملْ

If its dark around your
anus the natural sugars in
lemons help lighten it up

I hope you rot in
hell for what you
did.

I feel like those of us that
didn't delete the app are
part of some secret
community

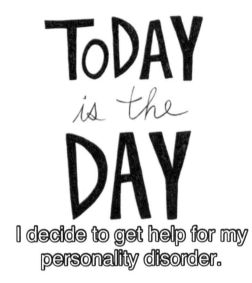

TODAY
is the
DAY

I decide to get help for my
personality disorder.

Bye

We are all connected , I
can feel it

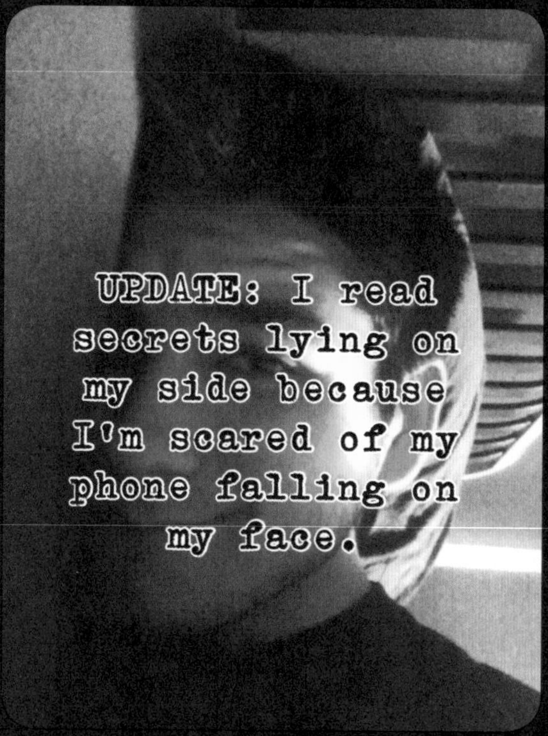

UPDATE: I read
secrets lying on
my side because
I'm scared of my
phone falling on
my face.

SURPRISES WITH THE PROJECT

What are some surprises you have had from PostSecret?

I have been surprised by how one secret or story can lead to another, then another. The courage to share a secret can be contagious.

My dad told me that toys grew under the weeds in the yard and if I pulled them, eventually a toy would pop out.

That endearing story was shared on the PostSecret Facebook page. It resonated with thousands of people who responded with their personal stories uncovering a whole subcategory of secrets: white lies told by parents—usually fathers—to their children.

My dad used to say that inside of the car's air bags was uncooked popcorn. When you wrecked the car the popcorn would pop and you would have a snack until help came.

My mom told me that chocolate milk came from brown cows.

My dad told me that when the ice cream truck plays music it means they've run out of ice cream.

When I was a little girl I was pretty fascinated with space. So some nights my dad would take his ladder and put it on our lawn and bring me outside to tell me he put the moon up for me. I believed him for years. He passed away a few years ago but every time I see the moon I think of him.

Secrets can make us feel isolated, but sometimes it just takes one person telling their truth to shatter the illusion that we are alone. The following letter started another chain of secrets on Facebook.

Hey Frank,

I am curious about orgasms and secrets.

I have had an orgasm horseback riding and have talked with other women who have also had them outside of any sexual experience, during everything from holding hands to an especially memorable shampoo and scalp message. Can you ask your followers to share their own stories about non-sexual orgasms?

Thanks!
Ashley

I've had them eating really good, really rich chocolate things—sometimes cupcakes, sometimes chocolate bars. I call them "chocogasms."

I can have them when I clean my ears with a Q-tip. I don't know what it is about the sensation but it brings me to orgasm nearly every time.

I'm a fifty-year-old male who can orgasm just by someone touching my breasts. It's automatic even now.

I used to get them while running. But only after going about 4 miles. People used to comment about my dedication to running. They had no idea.

Has happened to me a few times while meditating on God.

I was honored to be asked to deliver the graduation speech at St. Mary's College of Maryland. I went to the school in advance and handed out postcards to students. Each card had one question, but I didn't ask for a secret. Instead they read, "If you could share a one-sentence commencement address with your classmates, what would it be?" I was surprised when the question spread on Twitter and surprised again by the wise advice young people offered. I still do this for every commencement message I am invited to deliver, always including some of the thoughtful messages from the graduates in the finished speech.

Never be afraid of not knowing, it means you always have one more journey to take.

Don't live life randomly.

Be wise enough not to be reckless but brave enough to take great risks.

Couches become homes to raccoons if left outside all year.

Happiness does not come from money, it comes from compassion.

When you think you're about to have a breakdown, you're really on the verge of a breakthrough.

In the real world you must wear shoes.

I write erotic fiction about my coworkers...
University of Washington

When you were drunk you said you were going to marry me.

Just ask. The answer is yes.

I'm saving copies of my secrets in hopes that one day

someone will come along and I can trust them and me enough to share.

Sharing your secret with me shifted my whole world a single degree ~ to where it should have been all along.

I spent years lying about what an amazing husband he was, now everyone blames me for the divorce.

I made the mistake of complaining about my husband to my Mom. Now, there is NOTHING I can say that will improve her opinion of him. Sorry Honey!

THANK YOU

For not inviting me to your wedding.
I might have been the asshole that
stood up and said something.

I don't believe in love

I think

most

people

are

just

afraid of being

alone

Every Conversation..
When I'm on Vacation..
I have a different
            Occupation...
I take vacation from
            myself...

I ran out of hot water
shaving my pubic hair...

NOW   I'm

HALF   and   HALF

I was the one who threw the piece of pizza on the wall.

Life is **beautiful** and I'm ok. Nothing you've done or will do can change it.

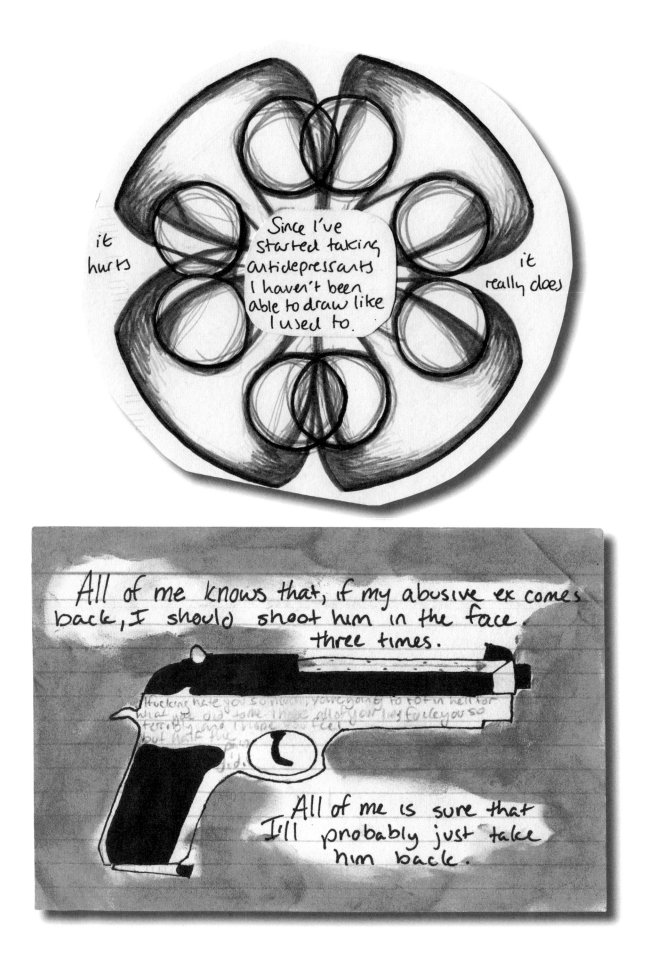

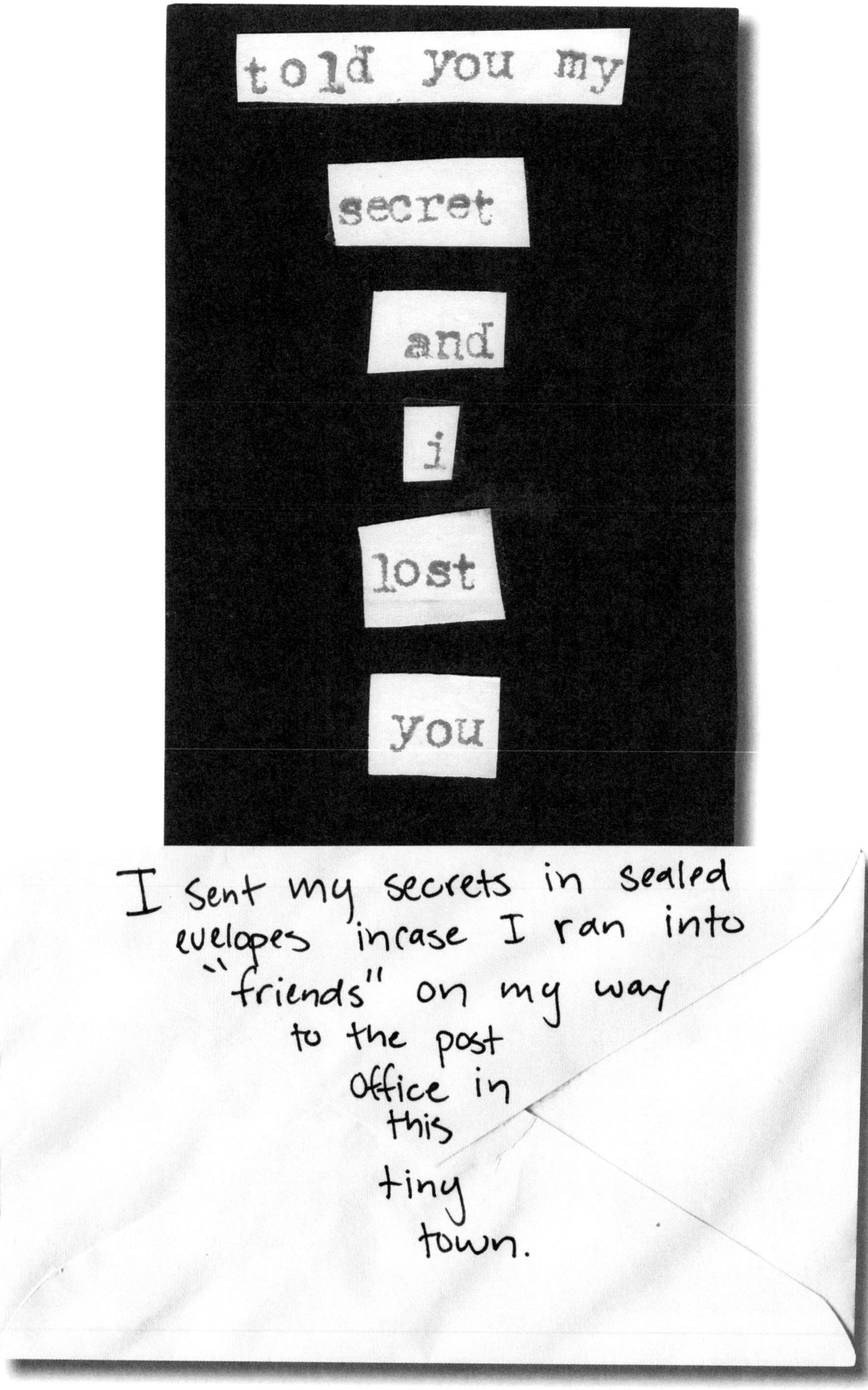

told you my

secret

and

i

lost

you

I sent my secrets in sealed
evelopes incase I ran into
"friends" on my way
to the post
office in
this
tiny
town.

I thought sending in one's **secret** would be EASY.

This is as far as I got.

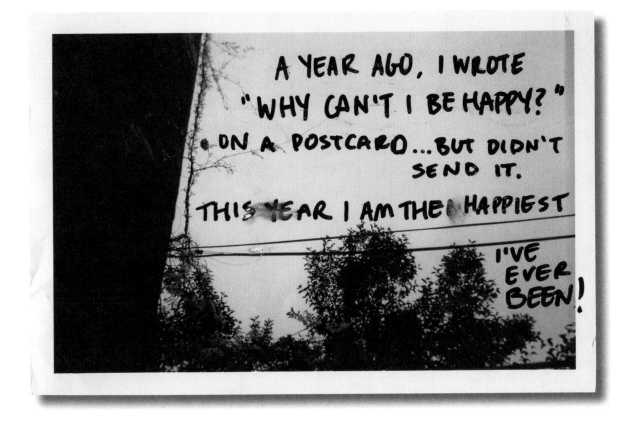

A YEAR AGO, I WROTE "WHY CAN'T I BE HAPPY?" ON A POSTCARD...BUT DIDN'T SEND IT.

THIS YEAR I AM THE HAPPIEST I'VE EVER BEEN!

NO ONE KNOWS THAT THIS WAS AN ENGAGE-MENT RING FROM MY EX...

IT FEELS ODD TO KEEP IT
IT FEELS ODD TO THROW IT AWAY SO MAYBE IT'LL HAVE BETTER LUCK HERE :)

Paris. © 1991 Succession Matisse

I am letting it all go. I am letting you go.
for good, this time. Good bye. Good luck.
it has been two years since I removed
I wore this ring for two years.

I NEVER MEANT TO HURT YOU.
BUT I NEVER TRULY LOVED
YOU LIKE I SHOULD HAVE.
I AM HAPPY WE ARE
DIVORCED.

AND I
FORGIVE MYSE
TOO
Mykonos
FIN

Here is your house Key. I will never need to use it again. Sorry for everything and... Thank you for the most am life experie

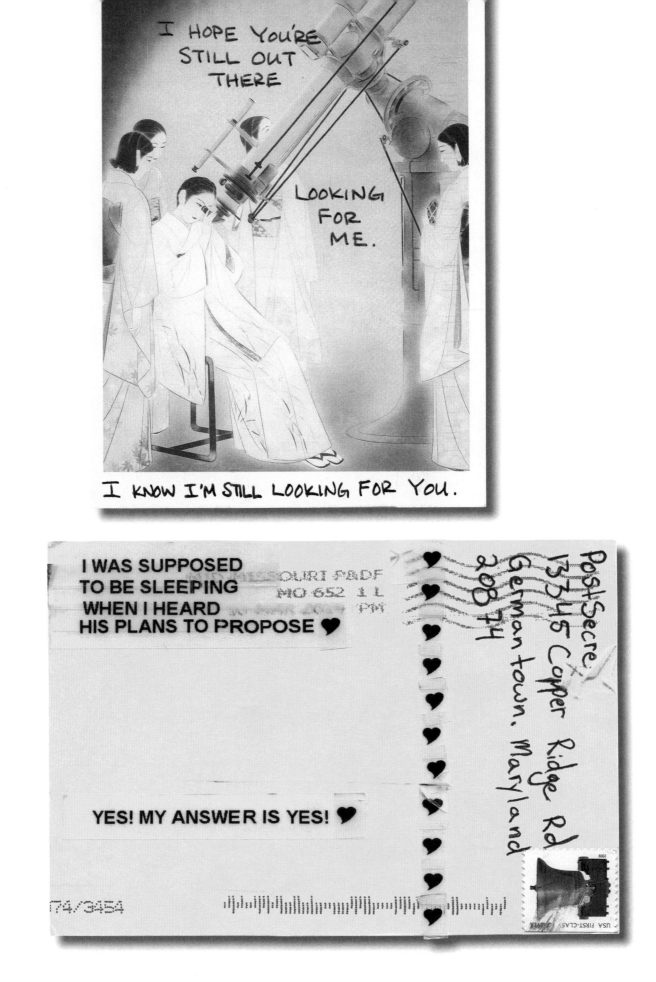

112

I HAVE WORKED IN AN OFFICE FOR 8 YEARS & MADE SEVERAL FRIENDS... NONE OF THEM KNOW I HAVE BEEN MARRIED FOR 10 YEARS BECAUSE I LIE AND SAY I AM SINGLE.

I wear flowery scents to work to keep my annoying, bossy, allergic coworker away from me. ☺

(and she thinks she's passive-aggressive)

WHILE PICKING A CARD FOR MY
COWORKER – I HAD TO AVOID

I see someone I admire

and respect in so many

different ways.

I see someone I'm proud to know...

someone I love sharing life with.

I see you...

THE MAN *I love*

HAPPY
Birthday

THE ONES THAT EXPRESS
HOW I REALLY FEEL.

HIS WIFE WOULDN'T LIKE IT.

BURIED SECRETS DON'T DIE; THEY RETURN TO HAUNT US LIKE GHOSTS OF OUR PAST SELVES.

My acupuncturist brushes my hair from my neck so gently... the way I hope a lover will some day.

OUR TIME TOGETHER

WAS THE ONLY TIME

I FELT TRULY HAPPY TO HAVE

MADE IT BACK HOME

I wish I dared to make the jump

+++ Berlin +++ Mauersprung +++ 15.08.1961 +++

- to move to the other side of the world

to be with you.

Massage Envy
SPA®

Gratuity

Thank you for your business!

To: I provide my own happy

From: ending after you leave the

Date: room to let me dress.

I'm stuck in love with my old boss.

We havent talked in months,

but he's still all that's ever on my mind.

I want to be strong enough to hate him for forgetting me.

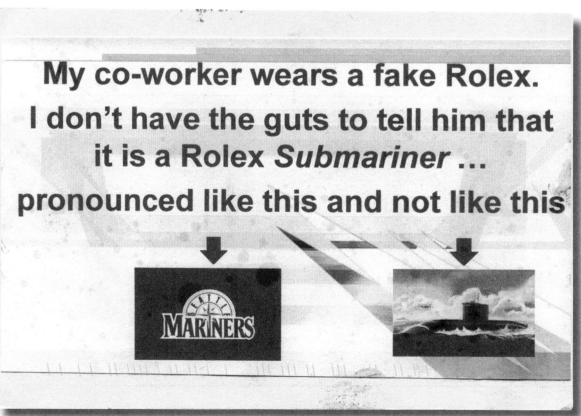

My co-worker wears a fake Rolex.
I don't have the guts to tell him that
it is a Rolex *Submariner* ...
pronounced like this and not like this

every time I
have to pee
really bad I
get super
horny.

THREE BATHING CUTIES, 1950's
PHOTOGRAPH BY RUZZIE GREEN

I can't face all
the "behind my
back" comments
from our co-workers.
That's why I
can't divorce him for you.

POST SECRET
13345 COPPER RIDGE RD
GERMANTOWN, MD
20874

U.S. POSTAGE
$0.32
80017
Date of sale
01/26/12
02 1P00
09241114

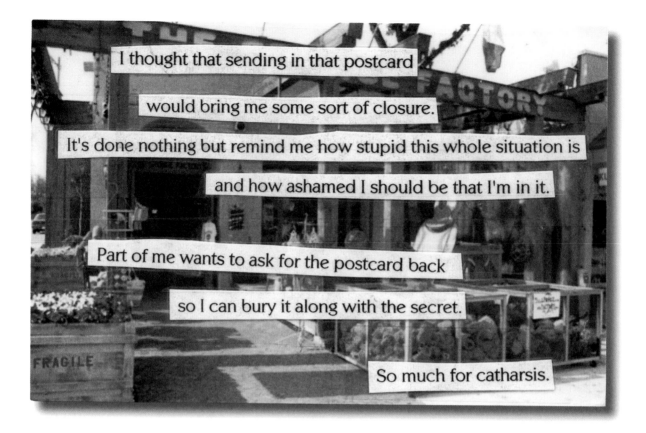

I thought that sending in that postcard

would bring me some sort of closure.

It's done nothing but remind me how stupid this whole situation is

and how ashamed I should be that I'm in it.

Part of me wants to ask for the postcard back

so I can bury it along with the secret.

So much for catharsis.

SUPERSTITION MOUNTAIN
ARIZONA PHOENIX
The Superstition Mountain, named for the legend of the
Lost Dutchman Gold Mine, are host to an abundance of
desert plant life, including saguaros, cholla, ocotillo cactus,
and yellow blooming brittlebush.

Photo © Paul Gill

I wish I had told
my deepest, darkest
secret to this fucking
post card insted of to
the love of my life.

Post Secret
13345 Copper Ridge Rd
Germantown, MD
            20874

DO NOT WRITE BELOW THIS LINE

13/12/12

I wish I was
as brave as those
that shared their
secret.

My secret is
Keeping me.

Postsecret,
13345 Copper Ridge Rd,
Germantown,
Maryland,
20874.

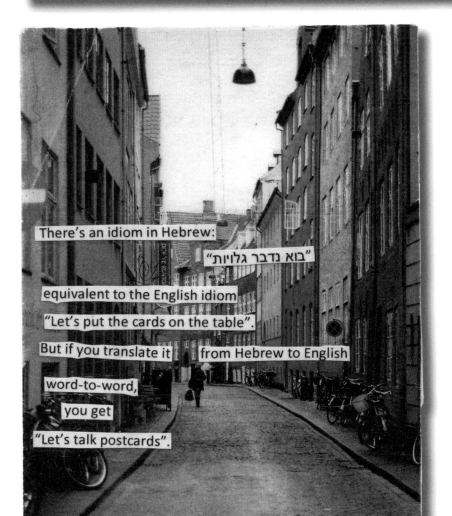

There's an idiom in Hebrew:

"בוא נדבר גלויות"

equivalent to the English idiom

"Let's put the cards on the table".

But if you translate it   from Hebrew to English

word-to-word,

you get

"Let's talk postcards".

Everyone who knew me before 9/11 believes I'm dead.

CONTROVERSIAL SECRETS

What are the most controversial secrets you have ever received?

Real secrets can make us feel uncomfortable. That's one reason people don't share them. Over the years, I have received some very controversial secrets and have been contacted by the FBI, various postmasters, and the police. I have received many angry e-mails and messages, some from my own family.

Surprisingly, the secret above with the Twin Towers did not generate many responses, although some people have told me it is the most memorable. One message I received came from someone connected with large-scale tragedies. He claims that in rare cases, people have been known to use a large disaster as an opportunity to start a new life and leave behind a looming divorce or escape imminent bankruptcy.

My brother doesn't know that his biological father is not the same as ours.
This secret was handwritten on a family portrait of two parents and five children. Family secrets can be very knotted. Who owns that secret? Would it be right for me to out that secret to the world, including the young man who was unaware of his own parentage? I have not shared this postcard.

I worked all my life to get into Harvard and now that I'm here I hate it.

The day after I posted this secret, the student who mailed it contacted me to ask if I would remove it because they had been identified on campus and it was creating new problems for them. I removed the secret and wrote back a short note expressing the hope that, in the short term, this disclosure may be difficult, but in the long run, it could lead to some healthy changes.

I made a secret covenant in the Mormon temple that I will never reveal the First Token of the Aaronic Priesthood, with its accompanying name and sign, and penalty.

Members of the Church of Jesus Christ of Latter Day Saints will tell you that the special ceremonies held in their temples are not *secret* but *sacred*. Either way, many Mormons were offended by a secret that displayed a ritual handshake and what appeared to be the inside of a temple rarely open to the public.

I made my cat drink bleach just so I could see my cute vet again.

This secret generated more angry e-mails than any other I have ever posted. Some of that anger was directed at me for "supporting" the secret. Sharing a secret does not mean I endorse or support it.

I said she dumped me, but really I dumped her (body).

This secret came on a postcard that carried a satellite image of a small unidentified patch of land. There were several interpretations of what this secret might mean. Some people believed it indicated that a body might be buried in the pictured woods.

Thirty minutes after it had been posted, members of the online community Reddit identified the location. Chicago police were notified and they investigated. A search of the site found nothing unusual.

I know this urban myth is untrue and faked. Yet . . . just imagining this picture REALLY creeps me out!

This secret arrived on a realistic photo of what appeared to be a woman's breast with a severe larvae infestation. Soon after I posted it, distressing e-mails began arriving in my in-box. People were nearly fainting or becoming ill just by viewing this image. I learned that there is a condition called trypophobia—a fear of objects with patterns of holes—and that people who suffer from it can have these very real physical reactions. If you are feeling brave or curious you can view this secret and a few more of the most controversial ones described on this page with the PostSecret Universe app.

When I'm home alone I cry and my dog looks at me, so I have to leave the room because I KNOW he's worried about me. I'm worried about me.

I'm so unbelievably thankful that it didn't work.

I wrote a suicide note when I was in seventh grade. No one knows. I hid it in a childhood safe and have since lost the key. I am terrified my mother will be able to open it one day.

This was suppose to be my last sunset

SHARED SECRETS REMIND US THAT FEELING ALONE IS NOT BEING ALONE.

I only feel

beautiful naked

in front of

my webcam

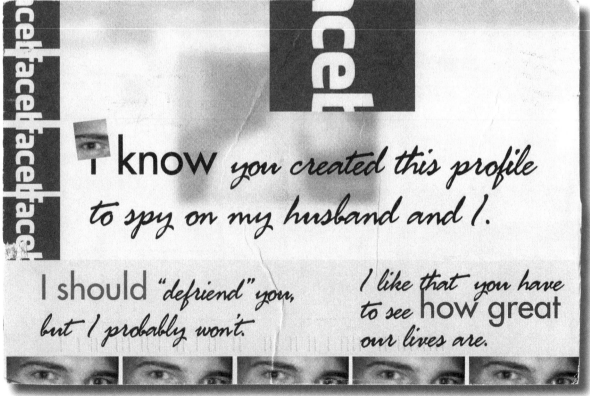

I **know** *you created this profile to spy on my husband and I.*

I should *"defriend" you, but I probably won't.*

I like that you have to see how great *our lives are.*

For the last 6 months...
After the kids are in bed,
my husband ignores me &
plays on his smartphone.

He thinks I'm working
from home at night. He
doesn't know I've been
chatting online with a
coworker.

I don't see this going
anywhere good...

I MADE A BOOK FOR MY BOYFRIEND
ABOUT "REASONS WHY I LOVE HIM"

I HAD TO GO ON THE INTERNET
TO GET IDEAS BECAUSE
I COULDN'T COME UP WITH
ONE REASON.

I STILL GAVE IT TO HIM. HE LOVED IT

So, have you figured out my secret yet?

01011001 01101111 01110101
01100001 01110010 01100101
01110100 01101000 01100101
01101111 01101110 01100101
01100110 01101111 01110010
01101101 01100101

49 20 73 74 69 6C 6C 20 6C 6F 76 65
73 6F 6D 65 74 69 6D 65 73 20 49 20
74 68 61 74 20 79 6F 75 20
77 6F 75 6C 64 20 63 61 6C 6C 20
61 6E 64 20 61 73 6B 20 6D 65 20
74 6F 20 6D 65 65 74 20 79 6F 75 20
68 65 72 65

B/C

B/C

PARIS
3.23.09

4.6.09

clyno
oayn
pa

dry

achaleym

dryd e

an

MMEMA
AMA
SIRTN
IA
AIMI   BARO

Joining my sorority saved my life.

ΣΣΣ

Alpha Alpha

"Faithful Unto Death"
won't be quite so soon ♡

I joined a sorority so I would have friends.

Alpha Delta Pi

Now that they have gotten to know me,

MEMBERS ONLY

none of them like me.

I FEEL LIKE

Ben & Jerry

ARE THE ONLY GUYS
WHO WILL EUER

Love Me.

FOR WHO I AM.

I am an animal rights activist

But I eat meat in hiding

I always thought grilled cheese, was "girl" cheese.

My mom told me I need to be careful and to watch what I eat because eating disorders run in my family.

I almost said "too late."

I'm sorry mom. P.S. I've been stealing your meds.

When my sister-in-law asks me to feed her dog, I sneak into her room and try on her panties... and... fantasize that she catches me and is turned on... and we have amazing sex...

When someone shows you who they are...

BELIEVE THEM!

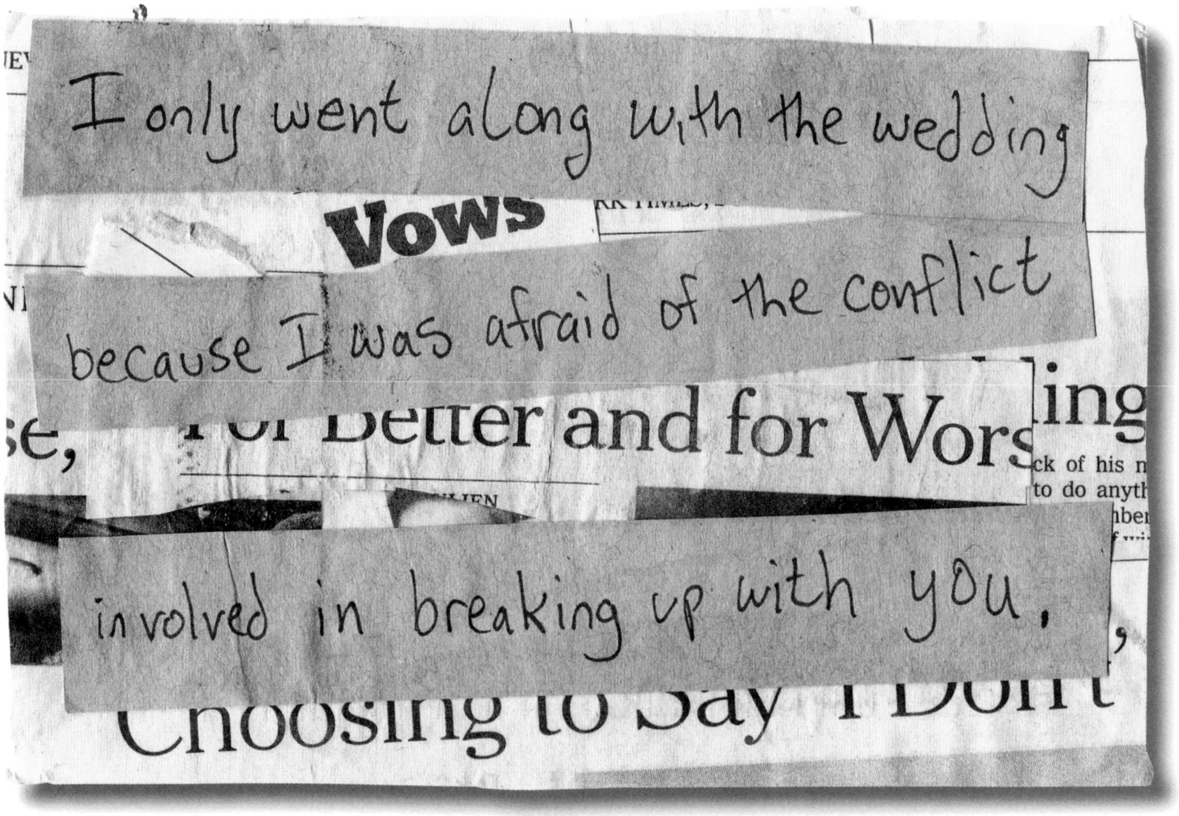

I only went along with the wedding

Vows

because I was afraid of the conflict

se, For Better and for Wors ing

involved in breaking up with you,

Choosing to Say 'I Don't

I'm a lesbian
but I'm in love
with a MAN

I'm _so_ confused

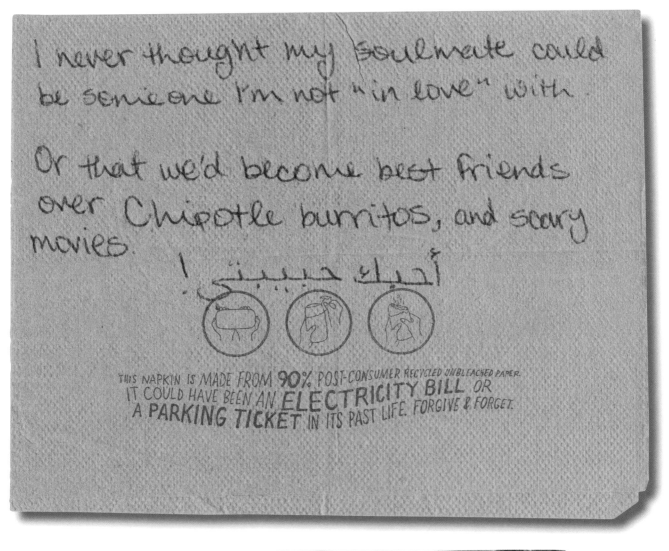

I never thought my soulmate could be someone I'm not "in love" with.

Or that we'd become best friends over Chipotle burritos, and scary movies.

أحبك جداً !

THIS NAPKIN IS MADE FROM 90% POST-CONSUMER RECYCLED UNBLEACHED PAPER. IT COULD HAVE BEEN AN ELECTRICITY BILL OR A PARKING TICKET IN ITS PAST LIFE. FORGIVE & FORGET.

I'M SO GRATEFUL HE ASKED FOR THE DIVORCE.

I WOULD HAVE STAYED AND BEEN MISERABLE.

THANK YOU FOR SETTING ME FREE!!!

There are days I would give anything

For someone to stare at me

like I was a piece of meat.

I noticed that since I had to stop mid-blow job and ask you for some water that there are now water bottles in every room of your apartment.

If there is one thing I will learn from my family, it is that no matter how old I get, they may never understand anything about me. and in order for me to be at peace with myself, I have to be ok with that. !:

I left my atheist group after realizing

the only thing worse than selfish, hypocritical

Christians

Are people who rant

about selfish and

hypocritical Christians

"Bothwell Castle"

...But never help anyone.

I'm not sure which bothers me more

birthday

Thinking she forgot...

wishes

...or thinking she remembered

Losing my baby was the best AND worst thing to happen to me

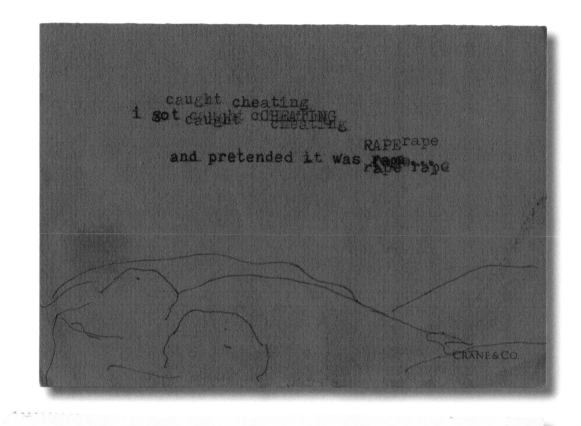

caught cheating
i got caught cCHEATING
caught cheating
RAPErape
and pretended it was rape
rape rape

CRANE&CO.

dear abuser,
keeping your
secrets nearly
ruined my life.

♡

I Believe in Karma

I Preach Love

I LIVE WITH
LOVING INTENTION

I Know a person
I WOULD KILL WITHOUT
REMORSE

"I'm 77 yrs. old
Today.! So much
life left. Secrets
go To the grave"

Frank
Now that you have read
so many secrets, do you
have any left in you?

YES ☐   NO ☐

MY OWN SECRETS

What do you do with your own secrets?

I have one of my secrets in every book, including this one. The first time I made a PostSecret postcard, it felt meaningful and weird to stamp it and mail it to my home. After it was delivered to my mailbox, I exhibited it with some others at an arts festival called Artomatic in Washington, DC. It was the first time I had ever exposed it. Anonymously watching strangers read it and react to it gave me the courage to tell my wife, and really let it go.

When I was in the Fourth Grade, a new kid moved into our neighborhood.

He was a charismatic leader who quickly became popular.

Soon after, he convinced two of my friends to pin me to the ground and hold open my eyelids.

They took turns spitting into my eyes.

Here are two more secrets of mine from the books.

Before I can use a public urinal I have to spit in it,
I don't know why, I just do.

I believe in a divine mystery waiting patiently
for our children to discover.

With each of the six PostSecret books I have tried to tell a different story. The second book, *My Secret,* was a book designed for the person I was when I was younger. In high school and at university I felt alone and struggled for direction. That second book was the one I wished I could have handed to myself when I needed to know that it gets better. This secret is mine. →

My wife has shared her secrets with me too. (She might get upset with me for retelling this one here, but hey, it's my job.)

My wife asked her friend if she had ever thought about divorcing her husband. "Yes," the friend said, and returned the question. My wife replied, "No," then added, "but I have thought about poisoning him."

THE CATCHER
IN THE RYE

J.D. SAL

If you feel like you are going insane,
and you are trapped in a
dysfunctional environment,
You Are Not Crazy.

I'm not the person I've always dreamed of being, but I love who I am more than ever!

On the road again!

We said we moved because of a job, but we really moved to get away from YOU!

We've Moved

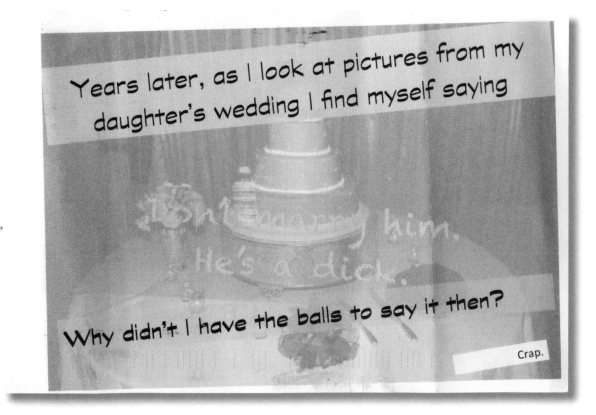

Years later, as I look at pictures from my daughter's wedding I find myself saying

Don't marry him. He's a dick.

Why didn't I have the balls to say it then?

Crap.

I HAVE A DIFFICULT TIME EXPRESSING THAT I LOVE SOMEONE.

BUT IF
I MAKE
YOU
PANCAKES...

(i love you)   (i love you)

(i love you)

(i love you)

THAT'S A PRETTY GOOD INDICATION THAT I DO. ♡

Many years ago, I was raped and almost killed. Instead of begging or screaming, I reached out my hand and asked "Did you come?" He dropped his weapon and left, and I lived. Since then, I have lived as if conciliation were key to survival. This was decades ago, but this has only just now occured to me.

For my father, my sexuality has become a battle for love between his God & his son. I just wish he had faith in me too.

I play old messages
just to hear your voice.

I miss you.

RECIPE FOR Disaster...

what if ...

HEALTHY START

* I write a recipe column ~

My Readers don't know about my

EATING DISORDER

151

last night
when you told me
how hott it was when
i spoke french
i told you how i'd
rather be fucking

your best **friend.**

il n'y a pas de qu

I

masturbate

with

vegetables

more often than I have sex.

My whole life I dreamed of meeting my birth family. I did when I turned 18!

They made me realize that my adopted family is my real family. Thanks for adopting me! You Rock!!

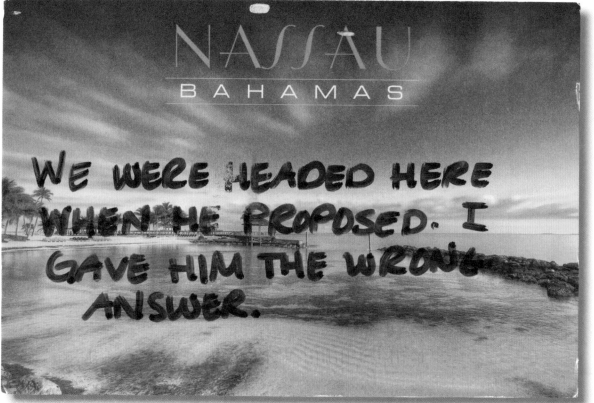

NASSAU
BAHAMAS

WE WERE HEADED HERE WHEN HE PROPOSED. I GAVE HIM THE WRONG ANSWER.

I HAVE MISSED OUT

ON SO MANY OF LIFE'S

NICE EXPERIENCES

BECAUSE I MARRIED

A FUCKING NUT JOB

I spent my preteen and teen years being bullied by my classmates...and my mother.
At one point I was planning my suicide. I couldn't take it anymore.
My mother read my diary (yet again) to see "what is wrong with you."
She read my thoughts and said, "Go ahead and kill yourself. See if I care."
That hurt more than her telling me I ruined her life by being born.
In a way she did save me because that's the day I planned my escape from all of them.

Does forgiving mean forgetting?

...and I did.

To anyone else that has lost someone, and now walks through life with a heavy weight on their shoulders, a vice of pain on their heart, horror in their veins, and an empty soul, wondering how you can possibly breathe another breath, get through another moment, with this as your reality. You are not alone

I walk with you

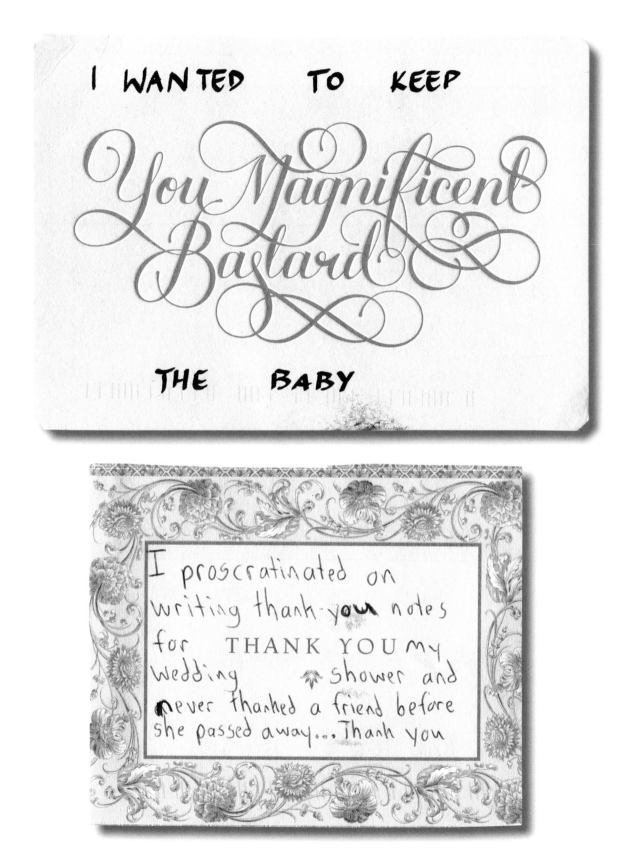

I WANTED TO KEEP

You Magnificent Bastard

THE BABY

I proscratinated on writing thank-you notes for my wedding shower and never thanked a friend before she passed away... Thank you

THANK YOU

Jaxon
Hudson
Trey
Roan
Dresden
Cruz
Trowa
Klynton
Cayne
Lorcan
Windyy
Oceane

Acea
Keetan
Adaer
Tayley
Kyler
Dokken
Declan
Ryker
Gage
Cullen
Grayson
Amory

I judge people for the stupid names they give to their children.

159

Sometimes I forget where I am and fart in public.

I convince myself that people don't recognize the sound.

But deep down I know.

The sad thing is, Kirkup said, "Suicide doesn't end the pain. It just passes it on to someone else."

This quote is the only reason I am still here.

Sometimes, people ask "If you could go back in your life, what would you change?" My secret is that I wouldn't change anything because, in the end, it took all the good and the bad to bring me here with you.

IS IT EASIER TELLING YOUR BEST FRIEND YOUR SECRET, OR A PERFECT STRANGER?

I didn't do it. well, nobody saw me. do it.

I am jealous of people who enjoy sex.

I miss falling in love.

...Being in love feels like a rut.

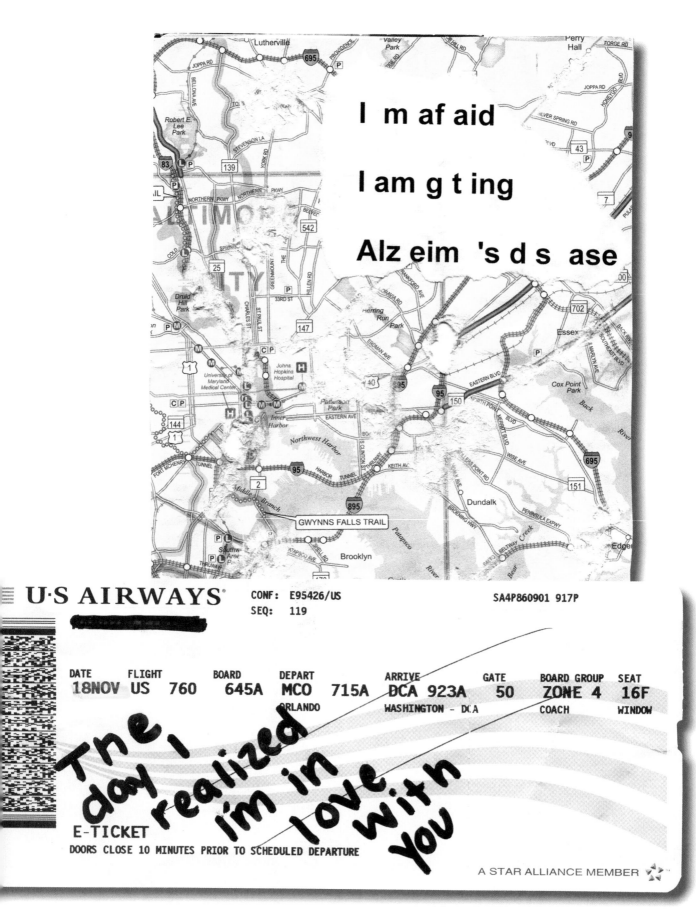

I m af aid

I am g t ing

Alz eim 's d s ase

US AIRWAYS

CONF: E95426/US
SEQ: 119

SA4P860901 917P

DATE	FLIGHT		BOARD	DEPART		ARRIVE		GATE	BOARD GROUP	SEAT
18NOV	US	760	645A	MCO	715A	DCA	923A	50	ZONE 4	16F
				ORLANDO		WASHINGTON - DCA			COACH	WINDOW

The day I realized i'm in love with you

E-TICKET

DOORS CLOSE 10 MINUTES PRIOR TO SCHEDULED DEPARTURE

A STAR ALLIANCE MEMBER

POSTSECRET FRANCE

postsecretfrance.blogspot.com

I learned many things throughout my time working on PostSecret France. But easily the biggest is that we can never know what is going on in the lives of others. Getting to peer into people's innermost secrets, ones that would never be uttered in any public (or even most private) conversations, was an eye-opener. It's made me much more humble, less quick to judge, and, ultimately, more empathetic.

One thing I noticed was that French people spend an inordinate amount of time concerned with situations of the heart. Most of the secrets I received had to do with relationships, and more often than not the positive aspects of them. I had always assumed that the stereotype that French people are more passionate about all things love was just that, a stereotype. But after doing this project, I can definitely see that "l'amour" (and all the emotions that go along with it) is a constant and driving force in the lives of French people.

I also learned just how awesome it is to get mail. And when I mean mail, I mean an actual, physical letter or postcard in your actual, physical mailbox. In this digital age, receiving a letter or a postcard (even if it is addressed to PostSecret France and not me personally) is one of life's little joys that, unfortunately, is being lost.

— BRIAN COTLOVE

I'm mailing this card because I get the feeling that I could meet the person who will change my life on the way to the post office!

J'aimerais avoir un pénis,

juste pour savoir

quelle sensation ça fait

KRAFT

Smooth~Crémeux

de le tremper dans un

pot de beurre de peanut.

I wish I had a penis just to know what it would feel like to stick it in a jar of peanut butter.

I learned French for you.

Mais je l'aime plus que toi,

AND I'M PISSED THAT IT WILL ALWAYS REMIND ME OF YOU.

POSTSECRET GERMANY

postsecretdeutsch.blogspot.com

PostSecret is a wonderful project, and I feel honored to be the German Secret Keeper. The biggest realization for me was that we all have a lot more in common than we think. Especially the part of life that many people consider "secret" is where we have a lot in common with others. We often fear, love, regret, and wish for the same things. No one is alone with their secret. Being able to post these secrets anonymously on the Internet and seeing other people's reactions to the artful postcards is a wonderful experience.

One such experience was when a stranger e-mailed me about a postcard on the German website. He was able to describe the reverse, which was not posted online, and he said he saw his girlfriend put the card into a mailbox. It said, "Run away!!! I'll only use you!!!"—"Renn weg!!! Ich werde Dich nur ausnutzen!!!" Once he confirmed she was the one who sent it, instead of running away, he asked her to marry him.

While we may think that secrets are what keep us apart from others, sharing them, even anonymously, brings us closer together. For me, that's the best part, and I hope that comes through in the German PostSecret book.

— SEBASTIAN J. SCHULTHEISS

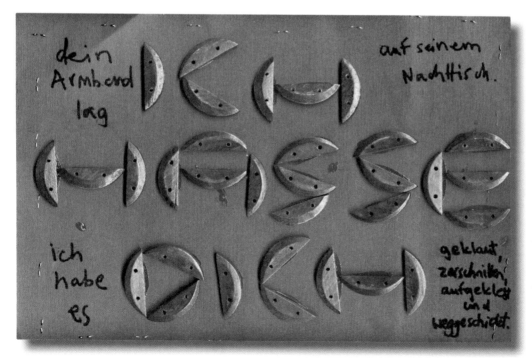

I HATE YOU. Your bracelet lay on his nightstand. I stole it, cut it to pieces, glued it to this page and sent it off.

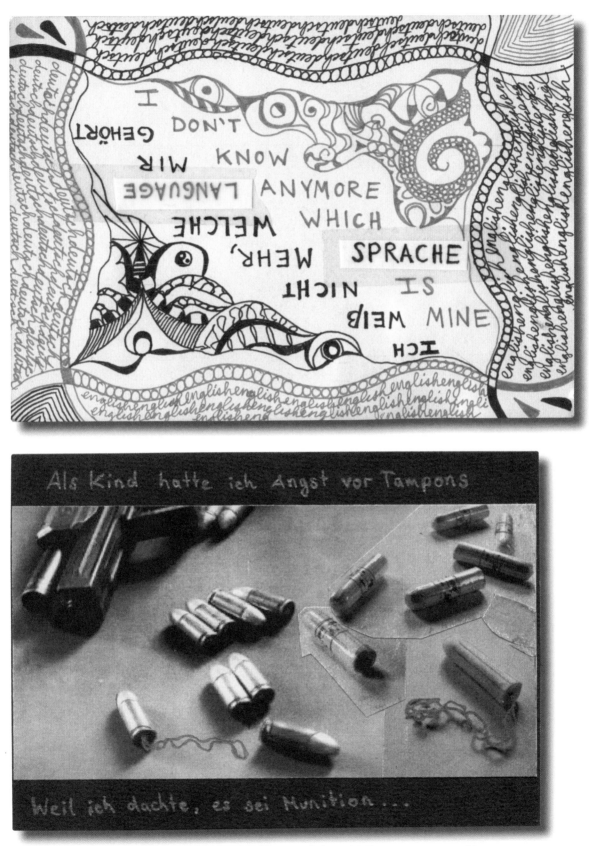

When I was a child I was afraid of tampons because I thought they were ammunition . . .

MY UNFORGETTABLE
CALL ON THE
SUICIDE PREVENTION
HOTLINE

There is a scene in the PostSecret play where you try to talk down a suicidal woman from jumping off a building. Did that really happen?

The scene is true and took place before I started PostSecret, when I was a volunteer on Hopeline (1-800-784-2433). You can read the whole story from the script below. We included it in *PostSecret: The Show* because of the connection in my own life between listening to anonymous callers talk about their personal struggles on the phone and reading strangers' secrets on postcards. In the play we dramatize this story and others that reveal the intimacy and healing possible between trusting strangers. The play also has many never-before-seen secrets, but be warned, you may hear your secret from the stage.

One Hopeline call I'll never forget began deep in the night with a polite conversation between a young woman and me.

The early part of the call sounds like the friendly back-and-forth that happens during a first date.

We develop a strong rapport.

She tells me she is hurting after a recent betrayal from a friend and feels alone.

I listen.

That's the most important thing we learned during Hopeline training:
    Don't judge.
    Don't try to be a problem solver.
    Create a safe space where a person can feel free to say anything.
    Speak with a voice of compassion, and listen.

Then she tells me, like she's whispering it in my ear, "I've been thinking about killing myself."

"Do you have a specific plan," I ask.

"Yes," she says.

I hear her walking around her apartment.

She tells me she's not drinking or taking meds, but her words are slurring.

Suddenly, I hear a loud thud.

I ask her about it.

She tells me she just slammed her sliding glass door shut and now she's on her balcony, sitting on the ledge.

"How many floors up are you?"

"Seven."

I try to keep my voice calm and reassuring, but my vocal cords are tightening and my pulse is racing.

"Will you promise me you won't take your life tonight?"

She doesn't answer the question.

I write down a request for my hotline partner to call our shift supervisor and 911.

Minutes pass, and I feel like we're making progress when suddenly she sounds scared and angry—someone's pounding on her front door.

I tell her it's probably the police.

"I sent them to help you. Is that okay?"

She stops talking to me.

I feel like I've betrayed her and lost her trust, like I've lost her.

My partner is in direct contact with the police and tells me that, because she isn't opening the door, the police are going to force their way into her apartment.

I tell her what's about to happen.

I hear them pounding . . .

I hear her sobbing . . .

I hear muffled voices that I can't understand.

My hotline partner hands me a note that reads:

"The police are in the apartment looking through a locked sliding glass door at the girl sitting on the ledge. She's jammed the door from the outside. Get her to open it!"

I can no longer hear anyone on the line, but I start talking on faith.

"I can feel the ledge you're sitting on because I've been there too. I understand why you don't want to unlock the door."

I tell her about the insomnia that pushed me to plan my death.

I describe how hard it was to open up to a psychiatrist and share my secret.

I explain how I was able to find my way through the pain.

And that talking to her, right now, is part of my healing.

I tell her, "You're saving me."

I ask her to stand up off the ledge, and as I say it I feel myself standing up from my chair.

My partner relays the information from the police that the girl is standing too, facing them, and walking back to the glass door.

My photography ...

has been lacking since I've started using hard drugs.

I ENDED UP IN A PSYCHIATRIC WARD BECAUSE I COULDN'T FORGET YOU

i am an abuse victim
a 9/11 survivor
I strugle with
waves of depression
im a child BROKEN
Down by the
world
and
I CAN'T
WAIT FOR
whats Next
Im more hopeful than ever

My kid is a drag.

There I said it.

More than 100 different men have seen every inch of my body and I have never met even one of them.

i'll never tell.

BY AIR MAIL
航 PAR AVION 空

we used to go shopping together!

Post Secret
13345 copper
Ridge Rd, German town,
MD 20874

I've kept a journal for my daughter since the day she was born.

I am afraid that I will die before she has any memories of me.

I NEED her to know that I love her with all of my soul.

I am trying to make sure that she isn't left with the same questions that I have of my own Dad...

I listened more than you think.

My dad has been dead for almost 10 years.

I still buy him father's day cards.

I remember more than you realize.

I forged my dads
signature on a DNR.
He died unwillingly.
Forgive me daddy!

I have forgiven my dad But I will never forgive myself for forgiving him

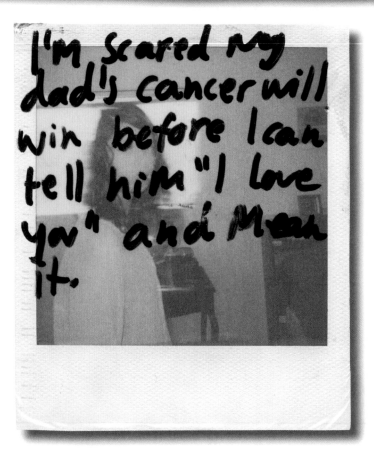

I'm scared my dad's cancer will win before I can tell him "I love you" and Mean it.

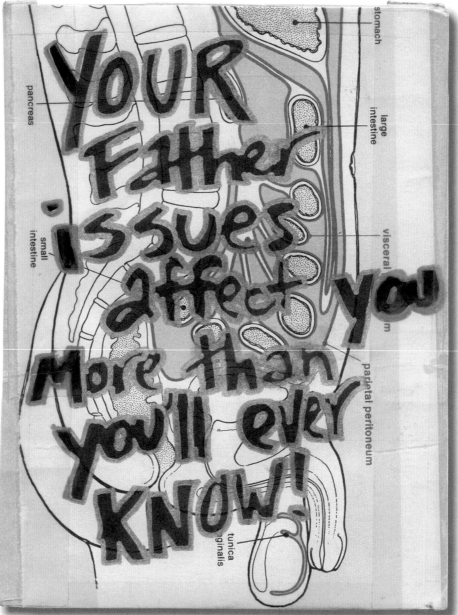

YOUR Father issues are affect you More than you'll ever KNOW!

ONE WAY TO HEAR YOUR CHILDREN'S SECRETS IS TO TELL THEM ONE OF YOURS FIRST.

I miss seeing you as the perfect Dad

I hope we can start again...

Eventually.

Today, I found out that the way my dad treats me is abusive, and I was told I am not the one with the problem.

I have never felt so much <u>relief.</u>

International Letter-Writing Week. 2013 国際文通週間

130 NIPPON

130 NIPPON

*0.90 DEUTSCHLAND

copper ridge road

60
75

POST SECRET

345 COPPER RIDGE RD.

ERMANTOWN,

MARYLAND,

NITED STATE OF

AMERICA 20874

Worl
up to

INMATE CORRESPONDENCE

RidgeRd
yland

THAT MY MAILMAN

KNOWS

성시 내손한로 132

www.usps.com

Air Letters

UI-WANG NAESON

의왕내손동

KOREA POST

28.04.2014

W660=

9g

[3지역]

To. POST SECRET

13345 Copper Ridge R

Germantown, Maryla

20874-3454

crets,
in
lease

CORREO AEREO

MAN, THAT FELT GOOD!

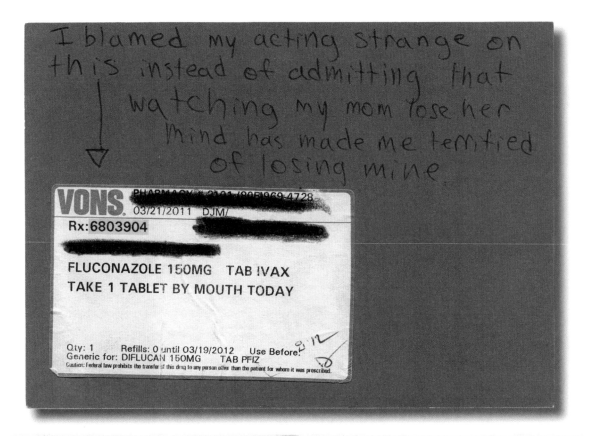

I blamed my acting strange on this instead of admitting that watching my mom lose her mind has made me terrified of losing mine.

VONS PHARMACY
03/21/2011 DJM/
Rx:6803904

FLUCONAZOLE 150MG TAB IVAX
TAKE 1 TABLET BY MOUTH TODAY

Qty: 1   Refills: 0 until 03/19/2012   Use Before
Generic for: DIFLUCAN 150MG   TAB PFIZ
Caution: Federal law prohibits the transfer of this drug to any person other than the patient for whom it was prescribed.

I AM REGRETTING MY DECISION TO KEEP MY PAST DRUG ABUSE ISSUES FROM MY CHILDREN.

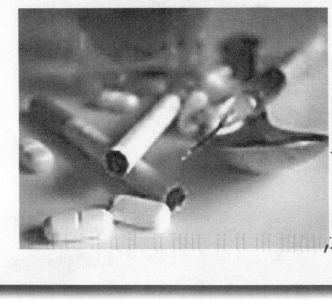

They deserve to know that they are facing an uphill battle genetically, but I am scared they will hate on me since I kept it from them so long.

My whole life my mom told me everyone else was mentally ill. I'm 30 and I just realized it's her. I feel like I'm abandoning her, and now she thinks I'm ill too.

Whenever I paint my fingernails RED, I only see my mother's hands

In fourth grade, I was the only student in my class who knew our zip code,

275487654876549756345309457894648056995647209387917385763
489560846784648695694140897960586280274-2974048756-
42709468034640874604846029411870764209146083463046307620
462946894756018972514637890205463782994543156278920345432
453647586954352435554678995448094657869994763524354675869
7065487362536478596076584763545364586976543546578697065984
because I would write to my mom in prison.

6578679675644356768456789034564872637849055432716526374854
960594873654235465786976548736524354657869786756554536458
769905876535465786790654736546578679685746335465786

I went grocery shopping right after I found out my Mom had cancer ....

I just wanted one last hour of NORMAL ....

May 19, 2000 / fri / 11:23 pm
"Being sick makes me loose
my energy, my impetus. I lead
a stupid life. Raising two kids
who hate each other. I suppose
that its an ok life."

I read your journals.
IM SO SORRY MOM.

When I was 20, I got a tattoo of John Lennon on my lower back. My mother was furious and told me that I'd eventually regret it. At the time, I told her she was wrong. Now I'm 23, and I'm sorry that I got it, but I don't want to have it removed because I'll have to admit that she was right!

We stopped for dinner on the way home from the hospital & missed a call from my Mum. I didn't call her back as I didn't want to wake her. She died **LOVELY!** that night. I will always regret not making the call

I was 9 when I told my mom my first real secret.

The next day she was discussing it on the phone with her friend.

I've never trusted her, or anyone else, with anything real since then.

except for you.

thanks for listening.

I Found this in a post secret Book

My mom is dedicated to her A.A. program. It drove me to drink at the age of 16.

I will never be as good as you tell your friends I am.

I FOUND THIS POSTCARD I HAD WRITTEN YEARS AGO, TO POSTSECRET, IN REFERENCE OF MY 'MOTHER. FOUR YEARS AFTER HER SUICIDE, I REALIZE I'VE WRITTEN A DIFFERENT STORY. ONE THAT ENDS HAPPILY.

I send cards to my friends on mother's day because they are such good moms and wonderful people.

I haven't sent one to my mother in 22 years.

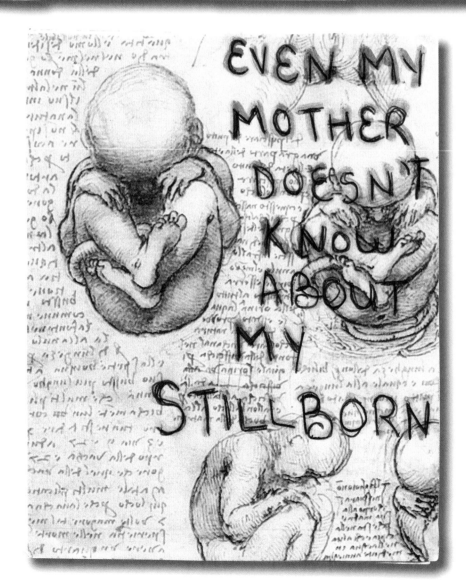

EVEN MY MOTHER DOESN'T KNOW ABOUT MY STILLBORN

A MESSAGE FROM MY
MAIL CARRIER, KATHY

Kathy was the first mail carrier for PostSecret and will probably be my favorite carrier for the rest of my life.

She no longer delivers the PostSecret mail, but here are some of her thoughts about bringing the world's secrets to my house.

As a mail carrier, you get used to seeing unusual things go through the mail. I have delivered ashes of deceased pets and humans to teary-eyed customers; tons of certified letters sent by bill collectors to equally teary-eyed customers; valuables in registered mail; live baby chicks, ducklings, worms, crickets; car tires and wheels; steamer trunks; and even packages that are broken and oozing unknown materials. You'd think I'd be immune to odd things. But nothing prepared me for PostSecret!

Frank, a customer of mine, started receiving a few postcards in the mail daily. They were preprinted with his address and looked like a card that a dentist office would send, reminding you of an upcoming appointment. It was just something I subconsciously noticed. There were just a few every day and they all looked the same. I never turned them over to look at the other side. That all changed one day for me.

While handling Frank's postcards, one fell out and landed upside down on the floor. I gasped when I read in huge bold letters **I LIKE TO HAVE SEX WITH STRANGERS**. You can imagine my shock. That's all it said. It had bright coloring underneath the letters. I'll never forget it. I immediately ran around showing my close friends what I'd found in the mail. One guy was so shocked, he said, "Did a girl write it?"

I was like, "How the heck do I know, who cares?"

I don't have to tell you that I may have pulled the few postcards that were in his address slot that day and begun reading them immediately! From that day forward, I (and a few friends at work who I'd showed the postcard to) may have begun reading all the cards daily. I still didn't really know what was going on, but I was intrigued.

A few weeks later I happened to meet Frank's lovely wife, Jan, at the mailbox. She had a knowing little smile on her face and looked as if she knew what I was going to ask. She explained that Frank started this little "experiment" a while ago, handing out these preprinted postcards at Metro stations and leaving them inside various books for people to find. Postcards were trickling in, but he really didn't expect much more from his experiment.

However, as time went on, the postcards began to more than just trickle in. They were silly, funny, serious, sad, lonely, hateful—every kind of emotion you could imagine on these little postcards. One of my co-workers said she couldn't believe that this person lived on *my* route. She said, "Of all people to get this on their route, *you*!" I took it to mean that she knew I was thoroughly enjoying it, and maybe she was a tad jealous! I have to say that it was fun and a great conversation topic, but despite all that, I began to learn from it. There are many sad and lonely people out there, and some of these postcards would break your heart. Suddenly the problems that I or my friends had seemed small in comparison. It certainly made me take a look at my life and realize how lucky I was.

By now I had also talked to Frank about his project. He came out to the mailbox one day and said, "I hope some of these postcards aren't too unsettling for you." I thought it was such a perfect statement, as some of them were very crude and he had to know that I was seeing them and possibly becoming offended. I assured him that I could handle it and thought the whole thing was a unique idea. Shortly thereafter Frank started a website for his cards. He began by posting several cards from his weekly bundle on the website every Sunday. And the whole thing just got bigger and bigger.

Soon I was getting postcards from overseas, homemade cards, extravagant cards that took hours to create. I remember one that had paper clips and office supplies taped all over it and said something to the effect of, "I hate my boss so I waste office supplies." So many people hate their bosses. I wish I could remember all the tricks that have been played on them. One of my favorites was from a person who wrote, "When I was a young man in Florida I used to work in a post office as part time Christmas help. We used to read all the postcards that came through. Do you all still do that?"

I don't know which happened first, whether the media got wind of the website or Frank put out his first book. All I know is that I rolled up in my truck one day and there were cameras and a reporter interviewing Frank by the mailbox. They were so excited that they happened to be there when the secrets were actually being delivered. I am camera shy (yes, believe me, I am), so I would never allow them to take pictures of me. However, many of them have pictures of my truck slowly pulling up to the box and my hand putting the mail in. I have been interviewed and asked all kinds of questions, like, "Do you read the postcards?" or "Does Frank treat you well at Christmas?" which I responded to with a resounding *yes* (even though we aren't supposed to accept tips. Yeah, right).

One asked me if I'd ever written in a secret. I actually *had* written a secret, but his question took me off guard and I suddenly felt flustered, as if somehow he would *know* which one was mine, so I told him no. Now I realize how silly that was. I never told that to Frank, I guess I should have. Anyway, Frank would stand by with a proud smile knowing that I was enjoying my little moment of fame. He'd go on a radio or talk show and my phone would start buzzing—"That guy on your route is on TV!" Then one day Frank got me at a weak moment and snapped a picture of me delivering his mail. The next book that came out had that picture right in the front! Was I ever shocked! But it was a fun surprise. My daughter was reading the website one day and clicked on a clip of one of Frank's speeches. She was amazed to see me up on the screen behind Frank. She said, "Hey, that's my mom!"

I actually *did* get a little fame from it! Some of the postcards started coming with "Hi Kathy" on the front. Frank has a large mailbox with a marker inside where people can come and sign his mailbox. There are a lot of messages written on it to me, thanking me for delivering the secrets. Frank even organized an Internet Christmas letter to me with messages from his followers online, and then he printed it out for me at Christmastime. I felt very special. He was always quick to acknowledge me as an important part of PostSecret. He has also given me all his books, signed to me by him, of course. He even signed one for my daughter. I have friends from other states who have e-mailed me and asked if there was any way that I was "Kathy the mail carrier" they'd read about on this new website for secrets they found. It's a small world, that's for sure.

I told Frank a funny story once. I was about a half mile from his house serving another customer one day and she asked me the "Are you the Kathy from PostSecret?" question. I told her I was and she was so impressed. She had just bought one of his books for her daughter, who is a huge fan of PostSecret. She asked me if I would sign the book for her. I told her I could do better than that—if she gave it to me, I'd take it to Frank and have him sign it. She responded, "Oh, no, I want *your* signature!" How funny is that? Frank was tickled when I told him that.

Sometimes when I arrived at his mailbox, there would be a postcard just lying in there that someone had driven to his house and dropped off for him. I often wondered if it made him nervous to have his address "out there" with millions of people. But he never seemed worried about it. One day when I got to the box, there was a note. I picked it up (I wasn't being nosy; a lot of times customers leave us notes to do something like go to the door to retrieve a package or whatever). To paraphrase, the note said, "Our parents think we are sleeping in the tent in my backyard but we took a road trip to see *your* mailbox instead!" It was signed by two girls from Ohio! Crazy!

Shortly after I retired from the post office, Frank had an exhibit at the American Visionary Art Museum. I was invited to attend but was traveling at the time. The art museum made me a bright-colored tiara with "USPS Wonder Woman" written on it. Frank sent it to me, and I will always cherish it. I wish I could have been there in person to accept it.

When I retired, the secrets were still coming fast and furious, and I'd read a few that happened to catch my eye. It has really opened my eyes to the lives of people all around you. There are so many stories behind the faces. If we could be as open to each other as the people who pour out their secrets, I think it would be a more understanding world. But too often people are afraid to show their inhibitions, sufferings, and well, their secrets. As long as we have PostSecret, there's an outlet for those who want to share. I have no doubt that it has been a good thing.

As happy as I was to retire from the post office, I was very sad to leave the PostSecret project and my friends Frank and Jan, their daughter, Hailey, and their wonderful, funny, lovable dog, Shadow! I couldn't have asked for nicer customers and a more interesting experience. I hope everyone who reads this will know how much their secrets meant to me over the years.

NO. 2008 ██████████

IN THE MATTER OF

██████████████████

AND ██████████████████

§
§
§
§
§
§

IN THE 211TH JUDICIAL

DISTRICT COURT OF

DENTON COUNTY, TEXAS

The "system" hurt me more than YOU ever did

MUTUAL INJUNCTION

On the _16_ day of April, 2009 the court considered and Ordered the following Mutual Injunction.

IT IS ORDERED that the following Mutual Injunction shall be effective immediately and shall be binding on the parties, on their agents, servants, employees, and on those persons in active concert or participation with them who receive actual notice of this order by personal service or otherwise. The requirement of a bond is waived.

IT IS ORDERED that ██████████████████ AND ██████████████ are enjoined from;

1) Committing family violence against the other party.

2) Communicating with each other in any manner.

3) Communicating a threat through another person to the other party.

4) From going to or within 200 yards of the residence, place of employment or business, or school of either party.

5) Harassing, stalking or threatening the other party.

6) The use, attempted use or threatened use of physical force against the other party.

Service of Writ

a Pelican Original   3/6

Sex in Society

Alex Comfort

I sacrificed my happiness for other people's. This is the first time I have said I AM GAY. I am 35.

MIDDLE CLASS

AGE - 47
OCCUPATION - SALES
SALARY - 52,000 + COMMISSION

WORRIED ABOUT LOSING THE JOB I DON'T LIKE. WHERE DID I GO WRONG?

Evelyn R

other evelyn@███████.com

other **Plot: N, 0, 2457**
San Bruno CA

Bill R

other bill@███████.com

other **Plot: N, 0, 2457**
San Bruno CA

I created email addresses for my dead
grandparents to tell them all the things
I never said. Now I send them pictures
of my kid so they can see how big he's
getting.   I still miss them.

I'M REALLY *excited* FOR THE DAY I CAN *unfriend* YOU ON FACEBOOK!

GRAND RAPIDS MI 495
OCT 2013 PM 2 L

Eliot Noyes
Typewriter   USA
ENERGY-EFFICIENCY
MONTH

Post Secret
13345 Copper Ridge Rd
Germantown, MD 20874

I should've been honest with you.
Of all people. But I wasn't because I was a pussy.
And I hurt you.
All you ever asked for was honesty.

You deserve more than just "I'm sorry."
You deserve a real apology. But I'm a pussy.

I miss you while I'm looking for myself out here.

WHEN YOU FIND YOURSELF you will find HOME

I am starting to like myself fully for the first time

Even the fucked up messy parts

Re-Reading the books we talked about

the perks of being a wallflower   STEPHEN CHBOSKY   BOOKS

JOHN GREEN   LOOKING FOR ALASKA   speak

made me fall for you... I miss you

zusak   THE BOOK THIEF   knopf

THE FAULT IN OUR STARS   JOHN GREEN   DUTTON

Nature and the Library are the only two places in America where I don't feel judged as "less than" because I am...

Quiet

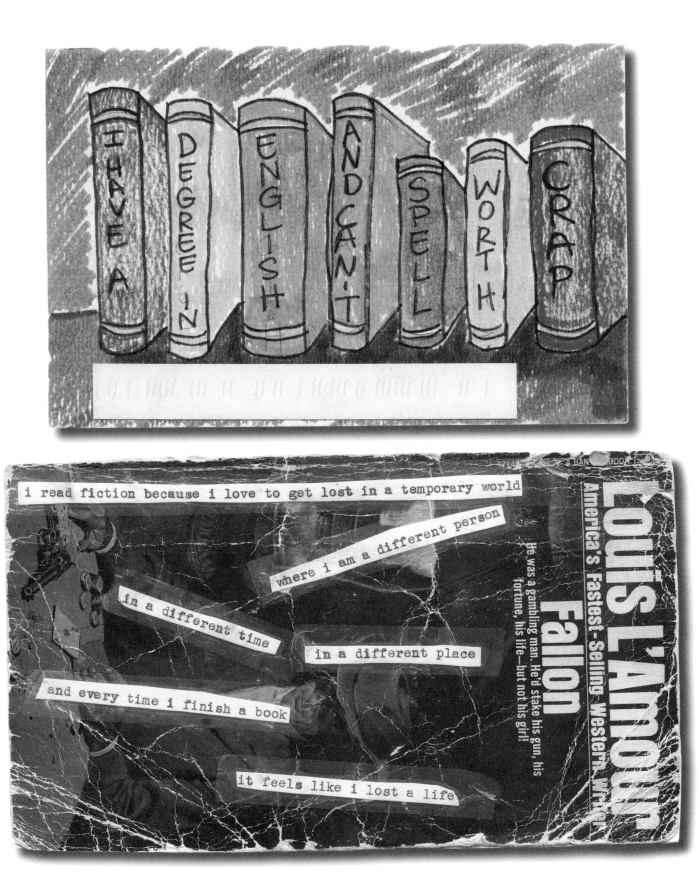

I HAVE A DEGREE IN ENGLISH AND CAN'T SPELL WORTH CRAP

i read fiction because i love to get lost in a temporary world
where i am a different person
in a different time
in a different place
and every time i finish a book
it feels like i lost a life

Louis L'Amour
America's Fastest-Selling Western Writer

Fallon

He was a gambling man. He'd stake his gun, his fortune, his life—but not his girl!

This is the week that I find out

if I have cancer

I don't know how to be this person

who doesn't get to expect

a full life

Vincent van Gogh, *Vincent's Bedroom at Arles*, 1888.
Rijksmuseum Vincent van Gogh, Amsterdam

PITTSBURGH PA 150

21 DEC 2010 PM 1

When I'm alone,
I want to be
with people.
When I am with
people, I want
to be alone.

Vincent van Gogh Book of 30 Postcards - BSB Publishing - The Hague - Holland

Postsecret

13345 Copper Ridge Rd

Germantown, Maryland

USA FIRST-CLASS FOREVER

0874+3454   20874

I'M
ALWAYS
WITH YOU.
I'M ALWAYS
YOURS.

you lied.

Sometimes
I like having
Cancer...

I feel less alone.

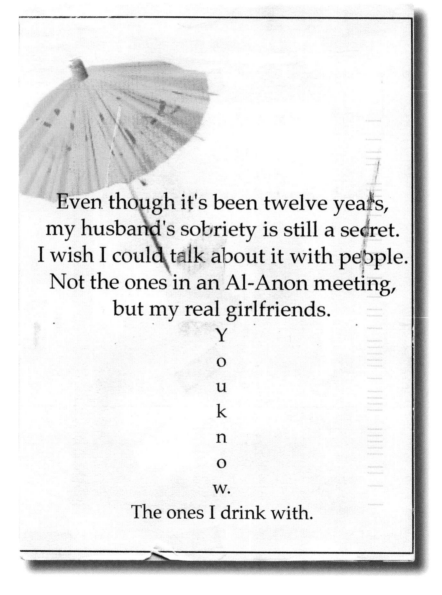

Even though it's been twelve years,
my husband's sobriety is still a secret.
I wish I could talk about it with people.
Not the ones in an Al-Anon meeting,
but my real girlfriends.
Y
o
u
k
n
o
w.
The ones I drink with.

EVERYTHING'S BOLDER WITH

GUINNESS

He's 25. I'm 23.

He just told me he's known for a year he wants to lose his virginity to me.

I don't know if I want that responsibility.

MIX BOLD BEERS

The employee-owners of New Belgium Brewing would like to thank the following for making our folly possible: the inventor of the bike, the Cache La Poudre river, our farmers and maltsters, the energy-stingy Merlin brew kettle, our five proprietary yeast strains, the Wyoming wind, the gazillion hard working microbes in our water treatment facility, our bio-generator, anyone who lives like there *is* a tomorrow, and everyone who enjoys our beer.

FollowYourFolly.com

If I stop being an alcoholic, I'm afraid I'll stop being me.

Post secret
13345 Copper Ridge Rd.
Germantown MD
20874

500 LINDEN FORT COLLINS, CO 80524 USA (888) NBB.4044

newbelgium.com

Printed on 100% Recycled Paper

Photography by John Johnston

DARK SECRETS CAN BE THE MOST ENLIGHTENING.

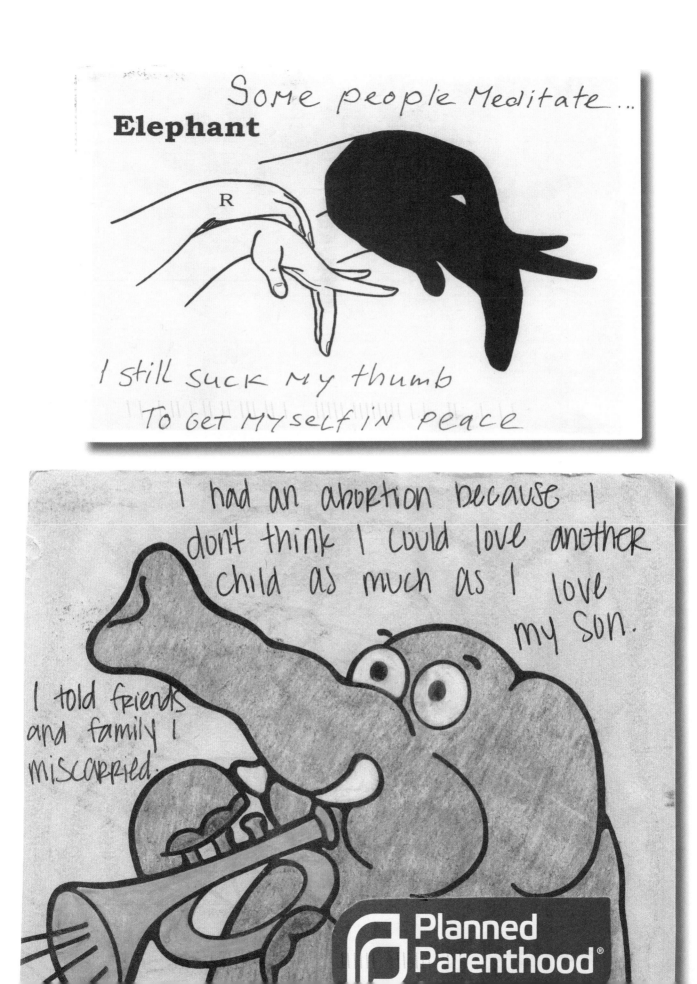

I am terrified I will develop Alzheimer's

and reveal to my children that I cheated on their father

for 12 years

I have never figured out if that was abuse

I have never figured out if that was rape

he drew this of me

I have figured out it is time to be my own muse.

IT'S HEALTHY TO SHARE MORE SECRETS THAN FEELS COMFORTABLE, BUT NOT ALL OF THEM.

A FAVORITE
POSTSECRET EVENT STORY

Do you have an unforgettable PostSecret story?

During a PostSecret Live! event in England, I projected some secrets from the PostSecret app on a movie screen for everyone to see. Some of the secrets had been created in the United States, but others had been made from people in the same neighborhood where I was speaking.

Even though the app is now closed, I am still able to search the archive by location and share secrets at every event that could have come from the audience.

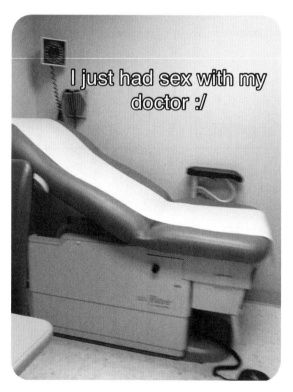

I just skipped class to sit by the window and stare out at the rain.

I'm the professor.

Today I found out my family secret. My grandfather was gay, and the only person who knew Was my amazing grandma. They raised a family together.
They were best friends.

Sometimes,
The Universe brings you to your knees
So that you can rise.
In the right direction

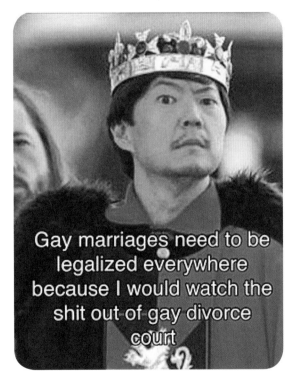

Gay marriages need to be legalized everywhere because I would watch the shit out of gay divorce court

Four of the app secrets I shared were created less than a mile from the Brighton Dome, where I was speaking that night. The first one showed a lonely street and told a painful secret, then two replies came from strangers, and finally, a "thank you."

"It's an illusion that we've been sharing other people's secrets. We haven't; we've been sharing our story, and now we all get to leave here tonight and decide how that story ends."

I ended the event with that line, then went into the lobby for a book signing. Sara was one of the first people I spoke to. She introduced me to her friend, who told me their story.

"When you showed my secret tonight, the one about wanting to be hit by a car, I went into shock. My gut reaction was to grab the arm of my friend and whisper, 'Oh my God, that's mine.' I didn't even think if I was prepared to admit it or not. I just did. But then I started feeling quite uneasy. I started shivering as I imagined what my friend was thinking about what I just confessed to her.

"After you said that final sentence, we got up to leave and my friend, Sara, leaned across to me and said that she was one of the people who had anonymously replied to my secret. I can't even begin to describe how that felt. 'Safe' is the best I can come up with."

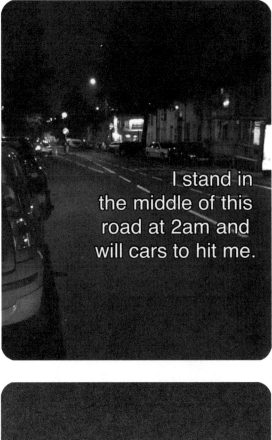

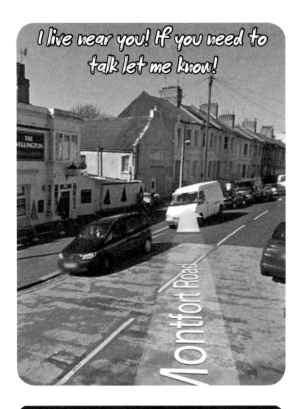

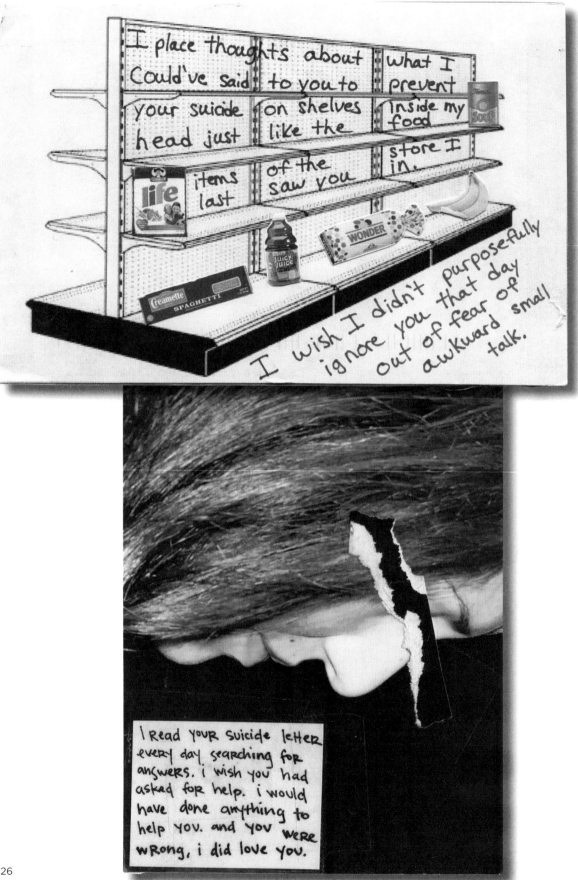

I place thoughts about what I
Could've said to you to prevent
your suicide on shelves Inside my
head just like the food
items of the store I
last saw you in.

I wish I didn't purposefully ignore you that day out of fear of awkward small talk.

i read your suicide letter every day searching for answers. i wish you had asked for help. i would have done anything to help you. and you were wrong, i did love you.

226

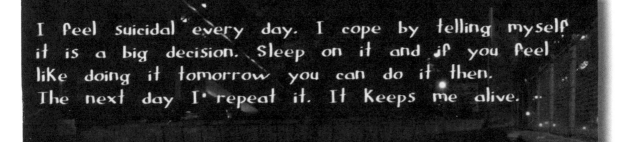

I feel suicidal every day. I cope by telling myself it is a big decision. Sleep on it and if you feel like doing it tomorrow you can do it then. The next day I repeat it. It keeps me alive. ..

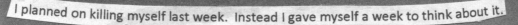

I planned on killing myself last week. Instead I gave myself a week to think about it.

It's been a week.

I've decided to live.

The world is beautiful and there is too much left unseen.

My girlfriend and I have the most stable, happy, functional relationship of anyone we know.

Just ask the girls we fuck.

I was teased and made fun of from K-12 for being "different!" NOW I'm a world traveling, well-respected glacial geologist.

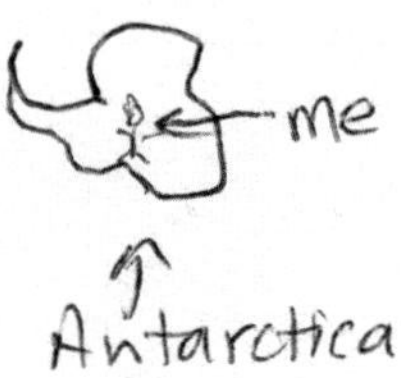

me

↑
Antarctica

If I could go back in time, I wouldn't change a thing, because what they said inspired me to be MORE! :)

P.S. Thank you

I ♥ YOU...

even though you'll never know it.

Secrets must be shared...
all over the world...
not just you.

— Hannah,
age 4½

THOSE WHO CLAIM THEY HAVE NO SECRETS ARE EITHER DECEIVING THEMSELVES OR US.

229

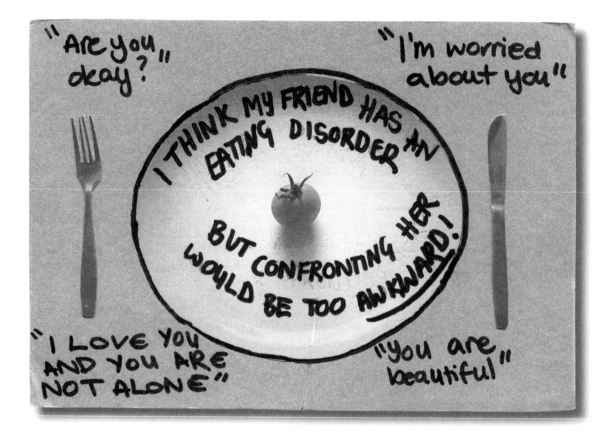

I changed my goal of weighing 120 pounds before I turn 30 to unapologetically loving myself.

He's getting fit because he wants to "be around for me for a long time"

I'm getting fit so I can leave him.

Run, run, run.
Run and jump.

"Faster, faster, Go faster!"

On March 28th it will be three and a half years since I made a promise to eat every day.

It's been a tough road but I've made it.

You can, too.

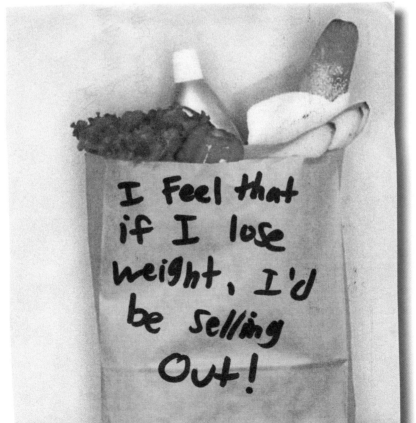

I feel that if I lose weight, I'd be selling out!

while packing things to put
into storage
          I realised I may never
unpack them —
          I don't think I'm
          going to make it.

As the sole survivor,

I still haven't figured out

if I was saved or punished.

I am <u>terrified</u> of receiving the phone call saying that <u>heroin</u> took your life.

Please stay clean.

I don't know how to tell you

I'm willing to risk everything

Don't love someone

to save yourself.

Love someone to destroy who you used to be.

for a chance to be with you.

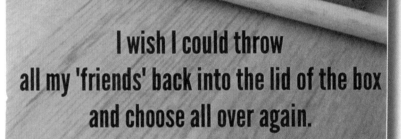

I wish I could throw
all my 'friends' back into the lid of the box
and choose all over again.

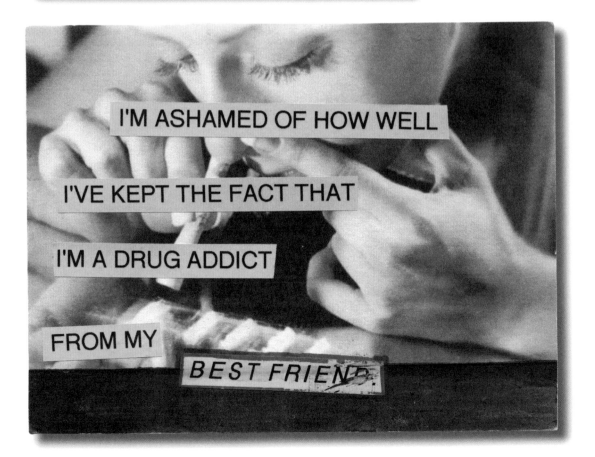

I'M ASHAMED OF HOW WELL

I'VE KEPT THE FACT THAT

I'M A DRUG ADDICT

FROM MY

BEST FRIEND.

I lie during therapy to

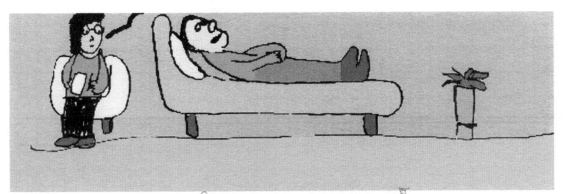

avoid the diagnosis I know they would give me.

The solutions to all of my problems are already in me...

I just need to find them

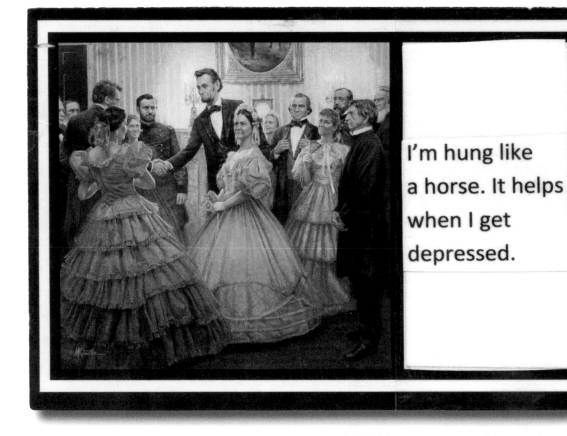

I'm hung like a horse. It helps when I get depressed.

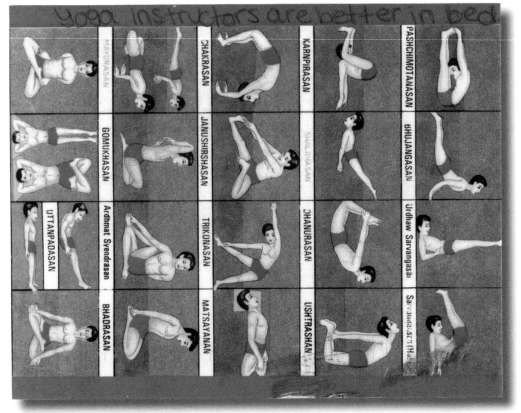

Greetings from California

Each time I use the laundry room at my apartment complex I leave extra Tide "pods" just in case one of my neighbors needs laundry soap.

I keep my Thank you cards in the same box as my sex toys...☺

thank you

1. I am the pianist at **3** different churches...
2. I don't believe in God.

have

God will take you on the greatest adventure if only you'll "say "yes."

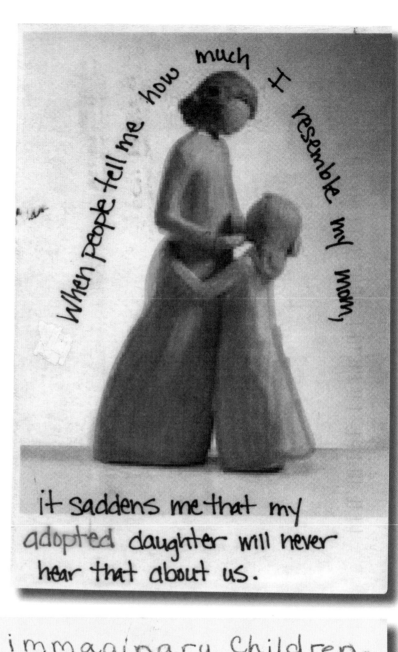

When people tell me how much I resemble my mom,

it saddens me that my adopted daughter will never hear that about us.

I have <u>3</u> immaginary children. <u>Evan</u>, <u>Lane</u> & <u>Lauren</u> turned 24 years old yesterday. I think it is time to give them up and face the fact that I'll never have kids.

It sucks being a gay man Sometimes

Love, Dad

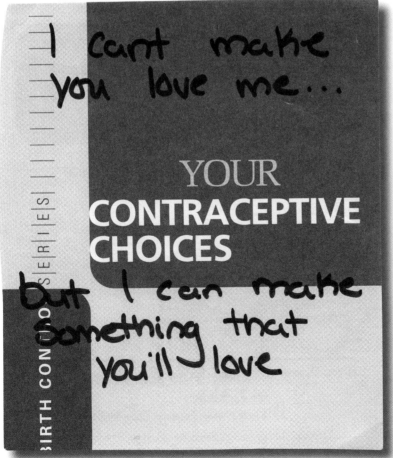

Sometimes we put up walls. Not to keep people out, but to see who cares enough to knock them down.

I saw this on the site and was reminded of something.

I had a secret... a big one, that had been eating away at me for a long time. I hadn't even told my therapist about it.

One night recently, I was lying in bed talking with the man I love, the man I'm going to marry. He mentioned his "walls" and opened up to me about them.

I was so moved by his trust in me and his love for me that I told him my secret... the secret I was never going to tell anyone. I cried and turned away from him, and he just held me and comforted me and completely accepted me for all that I was.

I might have mailed that secret in on a postcard one day... now I don't have to. It doesn't hurt me anymore.

Thank you.

– Alison from Minnesota

IS THERE A PERFECT SECRET?

What is the ultimate secret?

The first time I thought about an ultimate secret was before any secrets had been mailed to me.

One of the locations where I started PostSecret in 2004 was The Book Thing of Baltimore. It's a special place in Maryland where people can go to discover free books for themselves or donate new and used ones for others.

As I was leaving my invitations for secrets between the pages of books to be found serendipitously by strangers, I noticed a man nearby rummaging through the book stacks, obviously searching for something.

"Can I help you find anything?" I asked him.

"No, I'm not sure what I'm looking for," he said. "When I was a kid, I found this perfect book that changed everything for me. It opened my eyes. Now, I'm trying to find it again, but I don't remember the title or author."

"Well, good luck finding it," I said sincerely.

"Oh, I hope I never do," he replied. "Searching for it has brought so many other great books into my life."

Looking back on that story now makes me grateful for the life-changing journey my search for secrets has taken me on and for all the wonderful people I have met along the way. It also reminds me that later that day I wondered if there was a perfect secret, and if there were, what would it say?

Would the perfect secret help us better understand our own family secrets—the ones we kept and the ones kept from us? Would it be a bridge connecting us with others and our deeper selves? Would it be an answer to a question we didn't know we had? Would I know it when I saw it?

When the ultimate secret did arrive in my mailbox, I didn't recognize it at first because it didn't come on a postcard.

SHARE A SECRET

You are invited to anonymously contribute a secret to a group art project. Your secret can be a regret, fear, betrayal, desire, confession or childhood humiliation. Reveal *anything* - as long as it is true and you have never shared it with anyone before.

Steps:
   Take a postcard, or two.
   Tell your secret anonymously.
   Stamp and mail the postcard.

Tips:
   Be brief – the fewer words used the better.
   Be legible – use big, clear and bold lettering.
   Be creative – let the postcard be your canvas.

SEE A SECRET
www.postsecret.com

PostSecret
13345 Copper Ridge Rd
Germantown, Maryland
20874-3454

I hacked into my teacher's computers

to change my grades.

I graduated Valedictorian.

My former bosses will never admit it,

but I know I was fired

from my job at a Christian nonprofit

for supporting gay   rights on Twitter.

#SorryNotSorry   #LoveIsLove

Praying to a God I am not sure exists has helped me more than talking with friends/family ever has.

✝

my idea of heaven would be your HELL

I feel really uncomfortable around my husbands religious family.

I know deep down they think I am a heathen.

sometimes i wish i had embraced my muslim heritage

just so i could wear the pretty headscarves

and never worry about another bad hair day again!

THE SEX PISTOLS, LUXEMBOURG, 1977. PHOTOGRAPH BY © BOB GRUEN

I didn't know what
a secret was till
I admitted I was
keeping them from
myself

PostSecret
13345 Copper Ridge
Road
Germantown, MD 20874

MY MOM IS THE REASON I
DON'T KILL MYSELF.
AND I KNOW I
AM HER REASON, TOO.
WE HAVE NEVER
SAID IT, BUT
I KNOW WE BOTH
KNOW IT'S TRUE.

I find it extremely humorous when I can recognize food I ate in my poop (especially corn!)

HA HA

MY BOYFRIEND'S GRANDMA TOLD ME SHE LOVED MY EARRINGS. SHE DIDN'T KNOW THEY WERE MADE FROM SPARE KEYS FROM OUR SEX HANDCUFFS.

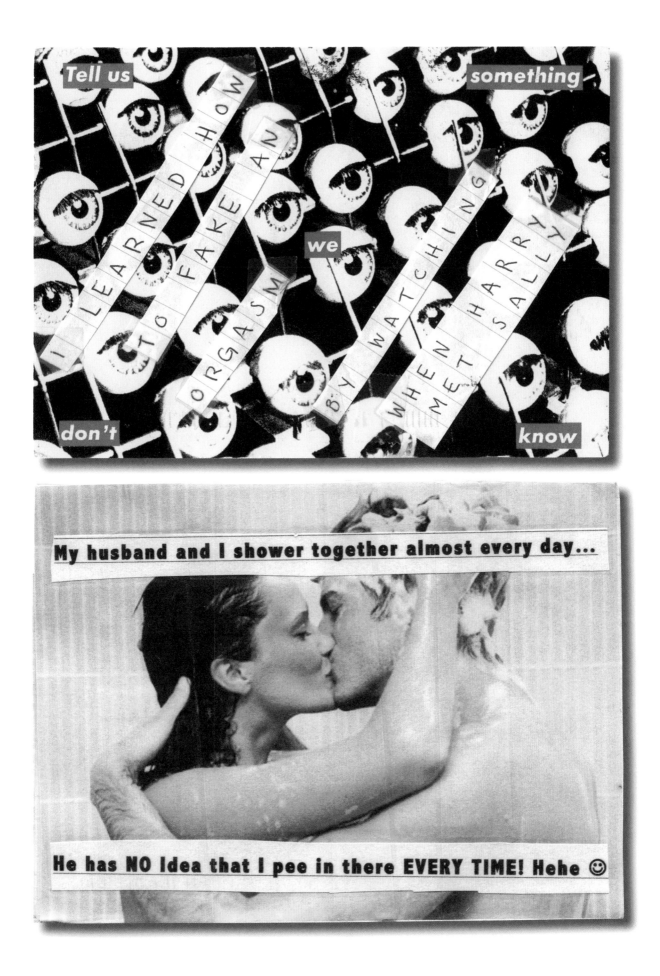

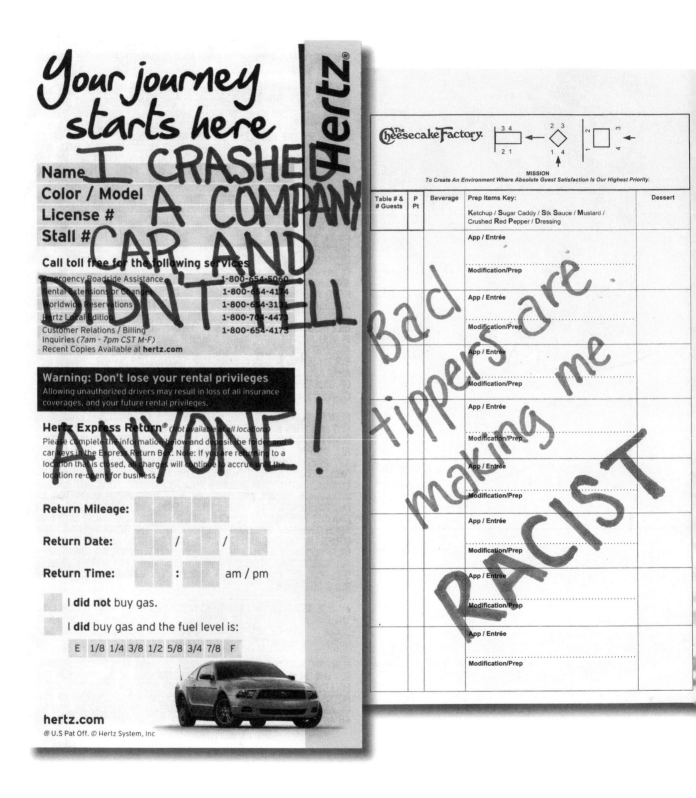

Your journey
starts here
I CRASHED A COMPANY CAR AND DIDN'T TELL ANYONE!

Name
Color / Model
License #
Stall #

Call toll free for the following services
Emergency Roadside Assistance   1-800-654-5060
Rental Extensions or Change   1-800-654-4174
Worldwide Reservations   1-800-654-3131
Hertz Local Edition   1-800-704-4473
Customer Relations / Billing   1-800-654-4173
Inquiries (7am - 7pm CST M-F)
Recent Copies Available at hertz.com

Warning: Don't lose your rental privileges
Allowing unauthorized drivers may result in loss of all insurance coverages, and your future rental privileges.

Hertz Express Return® (not available at all locations)
Please complete the information below and deposit the folder and car keys in the Express Return Box. Note: If you are returning to a location that is closed, all charges will continue to accrue until the location re-opens for business.

Return Mileage:

Return Date: /   /

Return Time: :   am / pm

I **did not** buy gas.

I **did** buy gas and the fuel level is:
E   1/8 1/4 3/8 1/2 5/8 3/4 7/8 F

hertz.com
® U.S Pat Off. © Hertz System, Inc

Bad tippers are making me RACIST

The Cheesecake Factory.

MISSION
To Create An Environment Where Absolute Guest Satisfaction Is Our Highest Priority.

Table # & # Guests	P Pt	Beverage	Prep Items Key: Ketchup / Sugar Caddy / Stk Sauce / Mustard / Crushed Red Pepper / Dressing	Dessert
			App / Entrée	
			Modification/Prep	
			App / Entrée	
			Modification/Prep	
			App / Entrée	
			Modification/Prep	
			App / Entrée	
			Modification/Prep	
			App / Entrée	
			Modification/Prep	
			App / Entrée	
			Modification/Prep	
			App / Entrée	
			Modification/Prep	
			App / Entrée	
			Modification/Prep	

On my 11th birthday I waited at my door for a letter from Hogwarts...

I was very disappointed.

I am seriously afraid that one of my ex-boyfriends will stalk and kill me.

The guy I used to hook up with ignores me because I fell in love with him.

Last weekend someone told me where he hides his house key

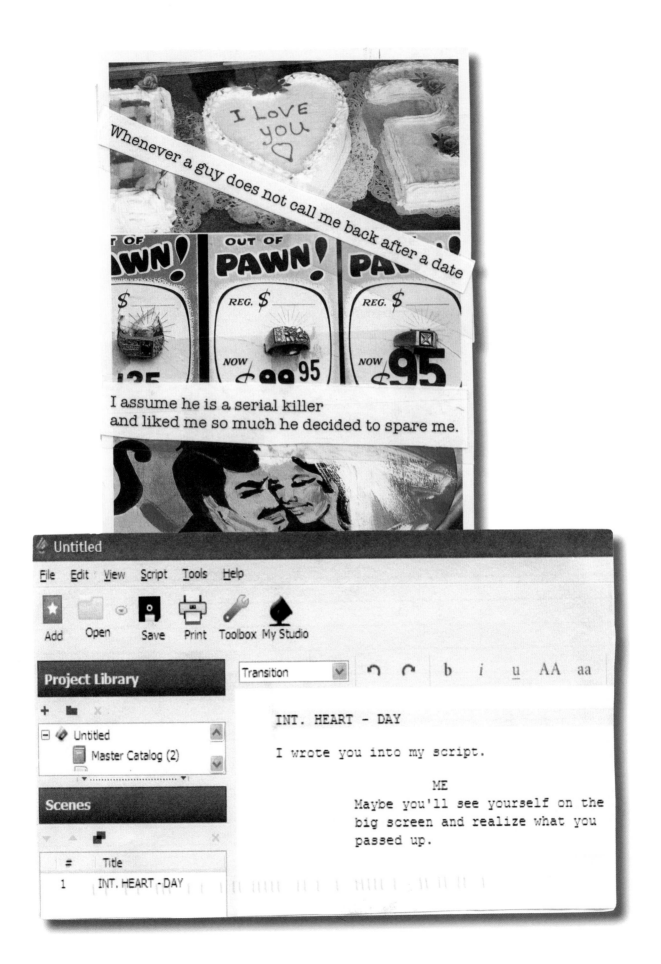

THE BEST LOVE AFFAIRS ARE THOSE WE NEVER HAD

Sometimes I wonder why did I ever meet you,
But most of the time I am just happy that our paths crossed.

I MET MY
SOULMATE ON
THE FIRST
TEE.

BRUISED HER
KNEE BY HOLE
NUMBER THREE.

I JUST THOUGHT
SHE SHOULD
KNOW.

National Hopeline Network

HoPE
1.800.SUICIDE
784.2433
www.hopeline.com

I'm scared to call.

I realized yesterday...
rather than an escape

SUICIDE

is a guarantee that this

suffering will last

For the rest of my life

Post Secret
13345 Copper Ridge Rd
Germantown, MD
20874

WHO KNEW APOLOGIZING TO HER WOULD SAVE ME FROM SUICIDE?

THE SECRETS THAT HURT TO TELL CAN OFFER THE MOST HEALING TO HEAR.

To the operator on the Suicide Prevention Hotline who took my call, You listened, you advised me, you calmed me, you didn't care that it might have just been teenagers hormones. You <u>Listened</u>. You were there <u>for</u> me!

Thank You!

You gave me strength to tell my parents and get help. You saved my life... and I don't even know your name. <u>Thank you!</u>

You don't know how much I want to meet you, thank you, and give you a hug!

265

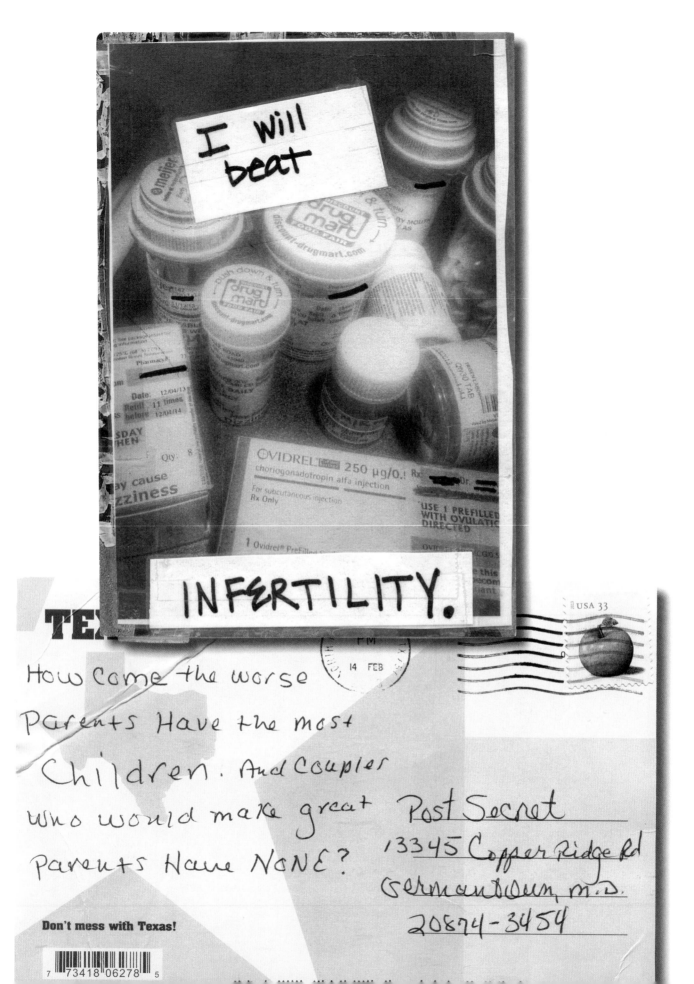

I make everyone I know think I hate children when in reality it's just a facade to cover up the heartbreak of not being able to have any of my own

I'M HOPING FOR A MISCARRIAGE

I once made a bet with my dad that I could solve a **Rubik's Cube.** After hours of frustration I peeled off the square stickers, rearranged them, and claimed my prize. I feel guilty to this day.

SORRY I PEED ON YOUR CAR DOOR HANDLE!

I FAKED
APPENDECITUS
TO GET OUT OF
SCHOOL...
I GOT SURGERY.

I can't
stand
ADULTS
and I'm
afraid of
becoming one.

These are secrets my students wrote a year ago.
My secret? I forgot to mail them.

just a note

I keep a photo of you and your wife to remind myself that you ARE happy with her.

I'm a democrat
an atheist
a vegan

so why am I
FANTA SIZE
about a

republican
christian
carnivore?

On my birthday, every year since I was 13, as I blew out

those candles, my one wish was to kiss a boy. On my 18th

birthday, I instead wished that you would beat your cancer.

One month later, I got my first kiss. It was perfect. You

have been cancer-free for three years. I haven't been kissed

since then. But still, I would trade in all future kisses if I

had a promise that your cancer would never return.

My Dad, my Mom, and my sister all tried to keep their first marriages a secret from their children. Between the three of them, they've had cancer five times.

I think secrets cause cancer.

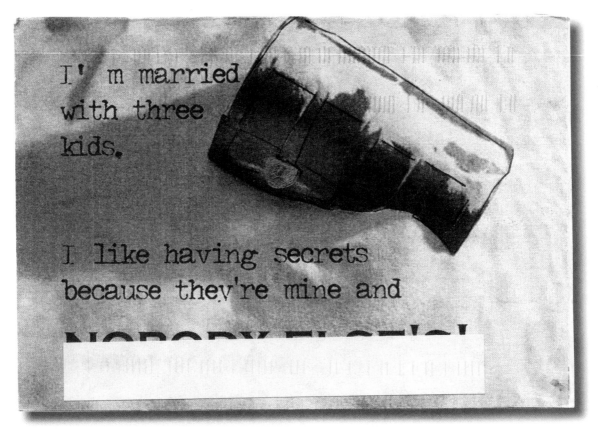

I'm married with three kids.

I like having secrets because they're mine and NOBODY ELSE'S!

I hate when the post office puts these over the last words of a secret

OUR MOST DAMAGING

SECRETS

THE ONES WE HIDE

FROM OURSELVES

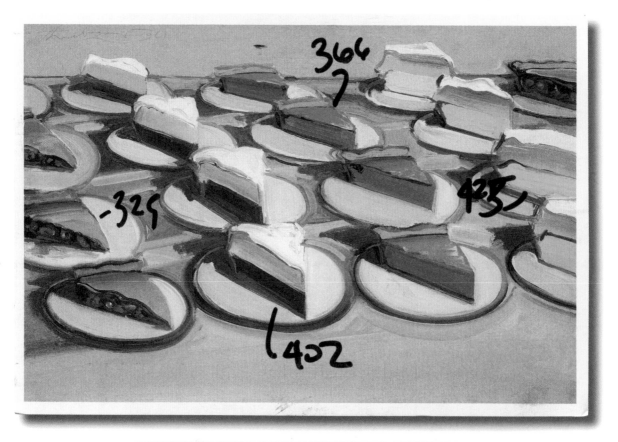

I FEEL PRETTIER WITHOUT MAKEUP ON.

I hate that leaving the house without makeup feels wrong.

I WANT TO FUCK THE GUY WHO BULLIES MY HUSBAND

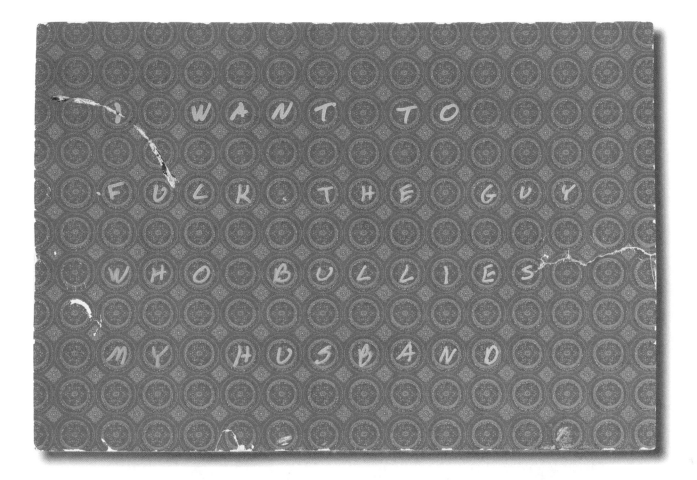

When I was in high school, I fantasized about getting even with the boys who bullied me. After I graduated, somebody did.

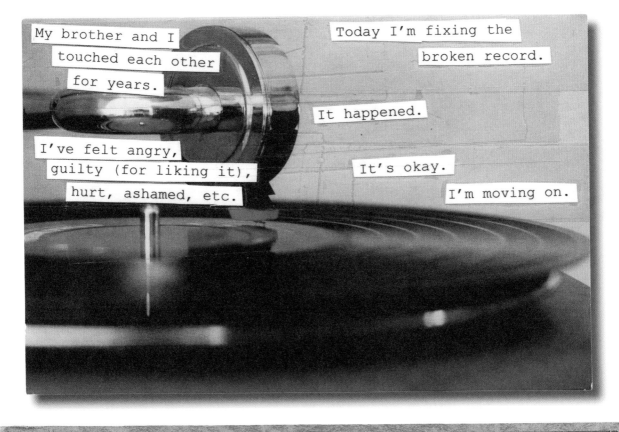

My brother and I touched each other for years.

Today I'm fixing the broken record.

It happened.

I've felt angry, guilty (for liking it), hurt, ashamed, etc.

It's okay.

I'm moving on.

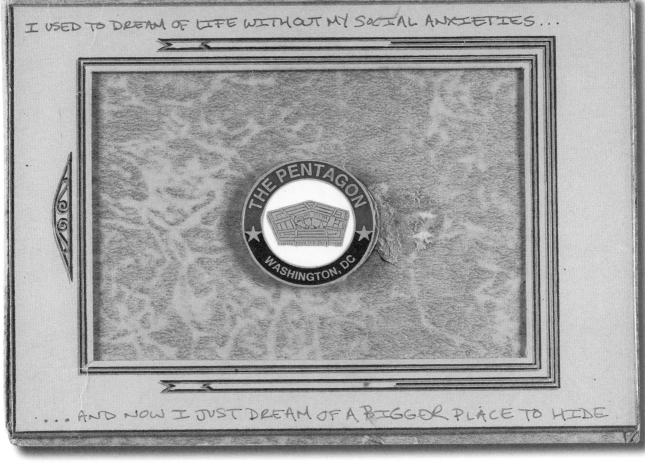

I USED TO DREAM OF LIFE WITHOUT MY SOCIAL ANXIETIES...

THE PENTAGON
WASHINGTON, DC

....AND NOW I JUST DREAM OF A BIGGER PLACE TO HIDE

Today is the day I declare
my independence.

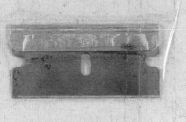

I'M ADDICTED TO T.V.

I HATE BEING A TEENAGER. PEOPLE ASSUME YOU'RE A THEIF!

Walmart Gift Card
gift card

2067493454

I JUST HOPE I CAN FIND SOMEONE, FALL IN LOVE AND SHARE ALL OF MY SECRETS WITH THEM.

I'm writing again.

My Fantasy life no longer sucks.

And my real life is getting better.

The first postcard I sent in made the Book.

I looked at it again the other day.

And I realized; my secret WAS NO LONGER TRUE.

Thanks, PostSecret.

I'm starting to feel FREE.

PostSecret
13345 Copper Ridge Rd.
Germantown, MD 20874

THE PERFECT SECRET

When I pulled the perfect secret from my mailbox and looked at it, I didn't understand it because it had no words. It didn't appeal to me initially as many postcards do. The ones that make an immediate impression on me are probably not what most people would expect. They can be funny and sad at the same time; they can be hopeful or reflect my own dark sense of humor. Here are three I'll never forget.

I steal small things from my friends to keep memories of how much I love them, mailed on a photograph of a photograph.

I WANT TO BE A SUPERHERO! I would use my power to take away your pain, written in red next to a woman in an action pose.

I hope your stupid wrapping paper collection catches fire and burns down your house, written on a postcard wrapped in Christmas paper.

The perfect secret was not mailed to me on a postcard. It arrived as a rolled-up painting canvas, but that didn't make it very unusual. This project has brought me dozens and dozens of personal possessions with secrets written on them. Along with postcards secrets have come on a mask, bra, flip-flop, watch, purse, and shirt. They've also been mailed on seashells, naked Polaroid pictures, a Utah license plate, certificates of birth and death, a sonogram, even an uncooked Idaho potato with my home address and postage right on the skin.

The painting of the young man and woman didn't seem that meaningful to me the first time I unrolled it. For me the most meaningful secrets come from strangers yet reveal secrets that we can see in ourselves. Maybe you came across one of your secrets in this book written in another person's handwriting. Or perhaps you felt less alone when you turned a page and saw for the second time your secret on a postcard you stamped and mailed.

I've had that experience. Looking back from a pyramid of postcards now taller than me, I can more clearly see some of the reasons I started PostSecret. I used to tell people I began collecting secrets because I was stuck in a boring career. That was partially true, but there

was a deeper reason driving me, one that I was unaware of at the time. I was building a safe community where anyone could reveal private truths because I needed to join and unburden myself.

As months passed I began to understand the perfect secret as being more than likable or meaningful—it was transcendent. It went beyond writing a secret and letting it go; it was about a place of trust, vulnerability, and courage where the reasons for keeping secrets disappear. It's something I can feel at PostSecret Live! events. I saw it in the PostSecret app and heard it as a volunteer on Hopeline. It's an idea I see in some of the private emails people send me, like these two:

Frank, I made a PostSecret postcard with a drawing of my fiancé asleep and a message about changing the alarm to spend more time with her. She found it before I could mail it to you and now we spend more time together while awake too. Thanks.

287

Dear Frank, I am going to buy a piñata and invite my friends to put their secrets in anonymously. Then we can blindfold each other, beat the shit out of it, watch our secrets rain down, and read them like candy.

For me the ultimate secret is this simple painting expressing that sacred space where secrets are never born between people or within our hearts.